BURPEE AMERICAN GARDENING SERIES

WATER GARDENING

BURPEE

AMERICAN GARDENING SERIES

WATER GARDENING

Ken Druse

PRENTICE HALL GARDENING

New York ◆ *London* ◆ *Toronto* ◆ *Sydney* ◆ *Tokyo* ◆ *Singapore*

PRENTICE HALL GARDENING
15 Columbus Circle
New York, NY 10023

PRENTICE HALL and colophon are registered trademarks
of Simon & Schuster Inc.
BURPEE is a registered trademark of W. Atlee Burpee & Company

Library of Congress Cataloging-in-Publication Data

Druse, Kenneth.
    Water gardening / Ken Druse.
        p.   cm.—(Burpee American gardening series)
    Includes index.
    ISBN 0-671-84645-0
    1. Water gardens.   I. Title.   II. Series.
    SB423.D78   1993
    635.9′674—dc20   92-7622
                                              CIP

Designed by Patricia Fabricant and Levavi & Levavi
Manufactured in the United States of America

10 9 8 7 6 5 4 3 2 1

First Edition

PHOTOGRAPHY CREDITS
Agricultural Research Service, USDA: pp. 90–91; Conroy, Mary Anne/Griffin, Steven L.: p. 6; Cresson, Charles O.:
pp. 60, 77 bottom, 78 middle, 86 bottom; Lilypons Water Gardens: p. 58; Pavia, Jerry: pp. 67 bottom left, 69
top, 81; Slocum, Perry: pp. 64 top, 66 top, 78 bottom, 80; W. Atlee Burpee & Co.: pp. 72 bottom, 78 top, 92

Line drawings by Elayne Sears
Horticultural editor: Suzanne Frutig Bales

Cover: *At Wave Hill, Bronx, N.Y., grasses and sedges fill containers in and around the
formal pool where Victoria lily pads hug the water's surface and tall pink lotus 'Momo
Batan' blooms.*

Preceding pages: *The pool and piped sculpture of a small boy become the subjects of a
floral painting in Ruth and Jim Levitan's Connecticut garden in spring.*

CONTENTS

INTRODUCTION

Nothing can match the power and majesty of water in the garden. Water catches light and traps it for a moment in a reflection, then lets it go so it can beam back to recapture the eye of the beholder. Does light fall from the sky or does it drift up from the diamond mirror nestled in the earth's perfect setting? Few additions to a garden, beyond its botanical wonders, can give as much as water. The water sounds soothe the soul; the plants and animals provide endless fascination. Your goal is to create a beautiful garden feature and a home for the things that live in and around the water. This book addresses many aspects of water gardening: location, pool size, construction, plants, animals and the information needed to develop and maintain a healthy environment.

A water feature can be made of any watertight container, from a ceramic urn filled to the brim, a tiny bubbling fountain playing the music of the falling droplets, to a large clay-bottom pond dug in the course of a natural stream. There, waterlilies and sunfish can be coaxed into sharing an afternoon with children who come for a dip.

Picture a pond filled with majestic *Nelumbo lutea*, the sacred lotus plant whose matte green leaves, nearly two feet across, sway in unison in the slightest breeze. This botanical sea of green rolls and tumbles like waves on the shore. In summer, perfect flowers push up above the leaves to offer their cups of gold. When you clap your hands, brilliant Japanese imperial koi come to the edge of the pool. These are treasured fish that will take food right from your fingertips. They are shimmering jewels of scarlet, platinum, ebony, gold and ivory. These carp relatives can live more than sixty years and grow two feet long—right in your own backyard pool.

Water gardening, perhaps more than any other aspect of our outdoor art, requires the gardener to simulate nature in microcosm. It's an environmental ideal created nearly overnight. It's an organic time-lapse movie—nature at high speed.

Just think: You excavate a hole in the ground, fill it with water, oxygenating plants, rocks and stunning waterlilies—all in two weeks. What would have taken nature years to accomplish, appears in a blink of the eye.

However, replicating the balance of the natural pool may take a little longer. When you fill the pool and introduce the living creatures, things might go well from the start. But sometimes the balance is distorted. There might be too much algae, exploding from all the sunlight that strikes the water. Fish waste, including carbon dioxide, contributes to this algal "bloom." Although this can turn the water pea-soup green, it isn't harmful to plants or animals, it's just unsightly.

After a while, the lily pads spread across the surface, shading the depths and causing the algae to fade. Underwater plants and the waterlily roots absorb more dissolved nutrients as they grow, starving the algae. The waterfall or fountain helps to settle debris and adds oxygen to the water, which also helps it stay clean. In time, with or without your intervention, the pool will find harmony.

Water is necessary for plants to grow—it is essential to life itself. We identify with its supportive familiarity. We should bring water to every garden. Think of it not only as an accoutrement but also as a giver of life for so many of the beings that share the earth. And the pool requires less water to maintain than a grass lawn. Any opportunity to create or restore a home for plants and animals, whether a rain forest or an inland waterway, must be embraced. Restoring a habitat, even a small corner of one, might be the most important contribution a person can make. A water feature, whether a formal fountain or a naturalistic pool in the shadows, is practically a necessity in the landscape. It is a chance to create a world in miniature. Imagine this contribution, and the life that teems in the watery habitat, the next time you see a puddle in the driveway.

The creeping rhizomes, leaves and flowers of the lotus plant Nelumbo nucifera *will colonize a pond that has a natural earth bottom.*

DESIGN

Water brings life to the garden, life to flowers in the pool and to moisture-loving plants by the water's edge. There is life in the movement of sparkling light. And, of course, there are the animals who live in the water's depth—ornamental Japanese imperial koi, perhaps, or fifty-cent goldfish, polliwogs and snails. If you're lucky, a frog or two will also seek the waterside. Birds will definitely come to your garden; moving water attracts them as much as any feeder. Birds come to bathe in the sun and drink while perched on a convenient rock, reaching down to sip some water and throwing their heads back to swallow with a shake and a shudder. These elements can grace your pool whether it be formal or informal, no matter the size.

Deciding what the water garden should look like comes first, followed by the intricacies of siting it (covered in the next chapter). Here, we'll concentrate on the shape, size and style. Sometimes ponds or fountains are the initial features to be developed for the garden; most often, however, the new water garden is in the form of a pool. A pool is a relatively small, manageable reservoir. A pond is larger, a fountain or tub, smaller and elevated, perhaps, and often with a built-in device that produces movement. Proportion is very important. The pool should be large enough to make a clear statement, and small enough not to dominate the landscape. Pools that are too small can be hard to maintain. The water may get too hot in the summer and become inhospitable to fish. I've found that water gardening is so much fun and collecting water plants and animals is so addictive that the pond never seems to be large enough. The larger pool, of course, requires more maintenance.

You'll probably choose to have a manageable water garden with enough space for waterlilies and fish. In order to support both fish and most waterlilies, the pool must be at least 18 inches deep. In USDA Zones 7 and colder, deeper is better. The practical limit to size is how much earth you are willing to dig and cart away. Later, you will have to be able to get into the pool to lower hardy plants for winter storage (refer to the individual plant portraits, page 57). Waist deep is good for a large pool 12 feet across at the widest part, in Zone 5, for example, where minimum winter temperatures can reach −20 degrees Fahrenheit.

You must strike a balance between your yard's size and design and the effect of the water element on it. Usually we think of a pool's design as either formal or informal. Rules say that formal gardens should have formal pools, and that naturalistic gardens look best with informal pools. This often is true, but it's a conceptual limitation perhaps best left undecided until all ideas have been explored.

A small, reflective round pool is the focal point of a formal town garden in Charleston, South Carolina. Its seductive interior color— black—creates a mysterious reflecting pool that appears to have no bottom.

FORMAL POOLS

Water flows out of a grotto, down a channel and into a formal rectangular pool in a decidedly Italianate setting at Blake Gardens in northern California.

Formal pools should have a permanent edging as uniform as possible. This is often made of slate or other stone, concrete pavers or brick. You might be able to find curved slate pavers for a circular pool. You can use square pavers and fill in gaps with smaller stones, but try to avoid the mosaic-tile look the English call "crazy paving."

If you think you would like a formal garden pool, you probably are picturing a formal garden. These constructions usually look best in geometric landscape designs. It is possible to site a formal pool in an informal naturalistic garden, but it is also more difficult. Formal pools are circles, squares, ovals or rectangles clearly delineated by coping—edging made of permanent, hard materials such as stone or brick—and paving. A square or round pool often is placed at the center of a formal garden and becomes its focal point. Turn a square 45 degrees and you have a diamond shape. Although the shapes are rigid and defined, there are variations that allow for creativity. Picture a series of circles, perhaps at various levels in the landscape. Water flows from one "bowl" into the next, connected by gutters and indentations, much like streams and waterfalls. Water spills over the edge of the highest circle into the next, and so on. Square pools might not necessarily be joined in sequence, but they can be connected. Imagine two large squares with a smaller square in the center. You could step across the pool from side to side by stepping across at the pinched square. This H configuration would work for joined rectangles as well.

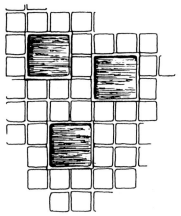

Formal square pools can be set into spaces surrounded by geometric paving. The pavers should just overlap the edges of the pools to disguise the liner sides.

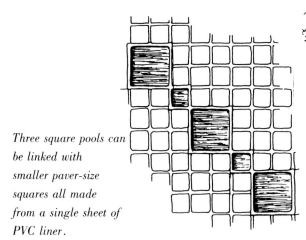

Three square pools can be linked with smaller paver-size squares all made from a single sheet of PVC liner.

A semiformal waterfall might be welcome in a formal setting. Instead of free-form, rocky water-holding receptacles, geometric basins may be round or semicircular, with water flowing over the edge of one container to the next.

A square pool may have its sides bisected by semicircles to create a design that is reminiscent of Islamic water gardens.

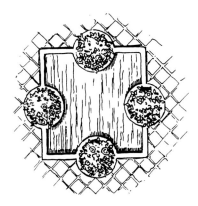

Round planting holes break-up the sides of a square pool, pushing plants, such as ornamental grasses, into the water area and surrounding pavement.

A crescent-shaped pool would be wonderful in a formal garden with semicircular benches artfully arranged to conform to the pool's shape.

A series of squares could also be placed within a limited area in a modern garden. A paved patio could be pierced by several squares of varying size. Or these squares could be set directly into planting beds; but remember, garden pools require frequent attention, and you must plan for convenient access —better in paved places than flower plantings with soil. The squares could be placed on the diagonal. Three squares running left to right, top to bottom, could be joined by two smaller squares.

An oval or oblong pool would also be good in formal plans. The long dimension should align with traffic patterns so that the flow of the garden is enhanced by the pool's design. Two oblongs laid perpendicularly over each other will form a symmetrical cross with rounded corners—a very attractive design for a central fountain, for example. Using a series of overlaid geometric shapes has unlimited possibilities. Picture a large square that has had its sides interrupted by semicircles. It would have a Moorish look. The square broken by semicircles is often found in Spanish gardens and Italian courtyard gardens.

A rectangular pool that enhances the overall shape of the garden can be very pleasing. The long, narrow garden could incorporate a long, narrow pool, leading the view toward an impressive flower planting beyond. A rectangular town garden could have a similarly shaped formal pool as its central feature, most likely located in the center of the garden, or it could be set perpendicularly at the far end of the garden to terminate the view. If the back of the garden abuts a wall, a fountain could be placed on the wall to pour into the pool beneath it.

You might try a *trompe l'oeil*, or "fool-the-eye" trick. The rectangular pool could become smaller as it recedes from the main viewing space, thus seeming to lengthen the garden. It would be best, however, not to exaggerate this too much or it might seem unrealistic. The fact that your eye can easily find fault is important when "drawing" a geometric pool in the garden. It is easy to notice when a circle varies in its uniformity. Bumps in the line of the coping or slightly oval circles will be easy to spot. Avoid a squashed

"Architectural" plants echo the formality of a pool's design. For example, Cyperus alternifolius, umbrella palm, in the pool at Blithewold Gardens and Arboretum in Bristol, Rhode Island, amplifies the structure of the rectangular pool.

A formal raised pool in an informal setting blends the best of nature and the gardener. This pool near Berkeley, California, is built of concrete—fine in a moderate climate.

At Skylands in New Jersey, the surface of the water is as important to this design as the wall, plantings or floating lily. It should not be filled with too many plants.

or misshapen appearance.

Water makes one want to linger, and a place to sit and while away the hours near a formal pool is something to consider. A crescent or half circle overlayed with a smaller circle could be made interesting with a bench in a similar shape. Consider the design of the bench from the outset, or, better still, plan it as part of the pool's design.

In all but the coldest climates, a formal pool can be elevated, at least partially, above ground level. A round pool could incorporate a coping at seat height (16 to 18 inches), so that one can sit on the edge of the pool and touch the water. Such pools are often made of reinforced poured concrete, but concrete block might be an easier choice. The texture of the blocks and the square edges could be joined, covered and smoothed with a coating of more concrete or stucco. Curved blocks could be used to make a smooth arc. The interior of the pool may be left as concrete or painted or fitted with a plastic or rubber liner (page 27).

When planning for hard-edge, formal designs, you must be precise. Draw the plan on graph paper and use a ruler and triangle for straight edges and a compass for circular pools and rounded edges. First draw your landscape, or at least the part of it where the pool will go. A surveyor's plan or house plans of your property would be useful, as the shape and measurements will all be in place. On an overlay of tracing paper, draw as many of the landscape features —flower borders, driveway, paths, trees and shrubs—as you can. At this point, you could cut out a scale drawing of the pool in cardboard or paper and move it around the designated area to see how it will "feel." Transfer the drawn design to the garden by constructing a grid of string tied to wooden stakes to scale. This grid functions just like your graph paper.

The drawn pool could suggest the scheme of an entire planting area. A round pool might become the center of radiating planting beds, a version of the old monastery gardens. Imagine a formal rose garden with a pool and fountain feature as its central element. Squares and rectangles might function similarly. In situations with informal, naturalistic pools, plantings go right up to the edge of the water and, often, into it. This is rarely the case with the formal pool. However, if you do wish to incorporate waterside plants into the scheme of the formal pool, you will have to plan for planting pockets, and these will have to work with the design. A rigidly formal pool can be installed in a naturalistic garden to counter and contrast its design. Just picture an overgrown birdbath or even a large concrete or stone fountain with grasses and flowering herbaceous perennials nipping at the base or partially obscuring the structure. (You could be creating the moment when nature begins to obscure the hand of humankind. This "ruin" would bring a wonderful antebellum romanticism to the garden. It would impart an air of gardens such as those in the interior courtyards of New Orleans.)

If you imagine again the square pool with half circles pushing out from each side, go a step further. These round shapes could be planned as half- or full-circular planters that break into the paved surroundings as well as the pool. Each circle could be planted with echoing formal plantings of nearly any plants, depending on your climate and sunlight and shade conditions. They could be formal annual plantings with verbenas surrounding spiky *Dracaena* in a Victorian style. Or you might design them so that they are simply shallow shelves in the pool to be a place to grow the "marginal" plants—those that grow in the shallows. Then these plantings could be of water canna, iris, sweet flag, arrowhead or other marsh plants.

If you want plants to grow directly in the pool, consider reiterating the formality of design by employing so-called architectural plants, those that have arresting foliage. The subtropical umbrella palm (*Cyperus alternifolius*) has striking stalks topped by whorls of straplike leaves. Combine this with the bold flat leaves of the hardy waterlily, which hugs the water surface, and you'll have a stunning effect. Try not to overdo these plantings. A formal pool that is overplanted may lose the intent of the design. If you really want to grow lots of plants then perhaps the formal pool is not for you. You might consider having more than one pool, or a blending of the styles: a semiformal pool.

The semiformal pool will have a specific shape and be surrounded by coping and pavers that make the shape hard-edge and permanent. However, these configurations would not be sharp circles or squares. It is more likely to be a kidney, hourglass, teardrop, horseshoe with planted island, footprint, or S shape.

If you construct a semiformal pool of concrete set into the ground, you may be able to create an overhanging curb that can hold soil and therefore lawn (or at least short groundcovers) could appear to go directly to the edge of the water. In this day and age, however, concrete is not often used for amorphous, free-form designs. And even swimming pools are not made of concrete much anymore; newer materials, often concretelike substances that can be sprayed on wire frames, are employed.

Herbaceous perennials and water plants have been "naturalized," encouraged to grow as though they were wild at "Flowery Brook" in the Montreal Botanical Garden, where the scope of planting was nearly unlimited.

INFORMAL POOLS

The inspiration for the design of informal pools predates the art of gardening; it is nature. If you are an avid natural gardener, you will probably embrace the informal pool or pond and wish to integrate it into the landscape's design. Plants, and in most cases animals, have to be considered from the outset. And you might not have a fountain or formal spillway—you'll have a waterfall. There, a stream (whether existing or constructed) will deliver water to the top of a rock construction where it will pool and overflow the edges of the elevated vessel, to fall, pool and spill again, as many times as space allows. The sound of falling water is one of the great

The rigid rim of a fiberglass liner creates a neat edge. This can be met by gravel or soil or pavers such as bricks. Although not an aesthetic welcomed by everyone, it is very effective here.

gifts you can make to a garden.

Although most naturalistic water gardens are small, even these can become realistic watery habitats, wetlands in miniature. The shape of an informal pool is usually irregular or free form, not geometric. It could meander a bit through the garden, changing size and form. Scale is as important as shape. You don't want to overwhelm the small garden, but neither should you create something that will be swallowed up by the surrounding plantings. The water feature has to become a part of the plantings.

The plantings around a natural pool are as important as, if not more important than, the aquatic plants within. Think of the woodland pond as an example and the waterside plants that line its edge. In summer, the edge of the pond is barely visible for the abundant shaggy

botanicals—marginal bog plants, ferns, grasses—that cascade over and often into the water.

If you live in a rural area and have a natural stream or an abundant water supply, you might consider having a pond dug. Your goal is to create something much as it would exist in nature. Consider making an island in the pond. The excavation could simply be made in the shape of a giant doughnut. Rock and soil could be left in the middle, or perhaps off to one side. You might decide to attach the island to the "mainland" with a rustic bridge. Plan to landscape the island.

It would be nice to have a simple soil edge for a small pond, but this is nearly impossible. Soil acts like a sponge, sucking water out of the pond or pool. And it can also slide into the water. Muddy water and muddy edging are always the result. A gravel or sand "beach" might work for a pond, but it will eventually be absorbed by the pond. In rainstorms, sand will wash away and gravel will become splashed with dirt. The gravel will also be hard to clean of debris such as flowers and leaf litter—especially if it is located at a place around the pond that has limited access. In the rural spot, a sand "beach" could be dumped each spring and raked smooth. This makes a comfortable entry to the pond for swimmers. It feels much better than slippery squishing clay between your toes.

An informal pool must be surrounded with edging just as a formal pool must; however, in this situation, the edging will be as free form as the pool's

Although the shape of an informal pool may be irregular, the edges will be clearly defined—usually with paving stones such as these cut "slates" set into brick.

design. Instead of uniform pavers, you'll select natural rocks. (Often the rocks will come from the excavation of the water garden itself.) The shape of the pool will undulate or at least weave in and out a bit. But be sure to incorporate places for planting from the outset. A shelf should be designed to go partway or completely around the inside of the pool (see page 29, Installation). Moisture-loving plants from the natural shallows can be grown in pots set on this rim that lies about 12 inches below the surface.

Consider also making two or more places along the pool's edge that jut into the main area of water for planting; likewise, similar indentations could bring the water to the surrounding garden. These can be small or large, enough for a single large plant or several; too small, they will destroy the naturalistic look of the pool.

Give thought to making a raised rock garden on one side of the pool with some of the excavated material, soil and rocks. A rock garden for traditional rock plants and alpines should be formed on the north side of the poolt it basks in the most sunlight from the south. You may wish to have a raised area that is more woodsy in feeling, perhaps dominated by small ferns and mosses. Its north-facing side should front the pool. Some shrubs or even small trees can be planted at the crest of the area to add shade for the woodland rockery.

The addition of a tree isn't out of the question, but be aware you may be creating a shady atmosphere. Evergreens have

less leaf drop, and if located to the north of the pool, their shadows will not fall on the water. Small trees such as dwarf Japanese maples would also be acceptable. There are also fastigiate or columnar varieties of familiar trees. Narrow, they grow up but not out, so shade is limited, and there are no overhanging branches. These, too, could be to the north of the pool. Dwarf flowering trees, such as crab apples or cherries, are spectacular near the water. The reflection doubles the impact of their seasonal bloom, and petals are sensational floating on the water. You may have to skim off the flowers occasionally, but flower drop doesn't last long.

Some of the excavated material could be used to elevate an area for a waterfall. This must be planned at the outset, but probably constructed when the major part of the pond has been dug and formed. The more planning you can do before you build the pool, the better. It is not unrealistic to choose some of the plants in advance from catalogs and books. Remember to consider not only the needs of the plants as to sun and moisture but also their ultimate size. It is easy for some aquatic plants to cover the top of the water completely. Also, many herbaceous perennials that look especially nice next to the water, for example *Rodgersia* and certain large hostas whose broad leaves lend a decidedly tropical feeling to the pool, might grow too big for a small pool. A plant that is half as big as the pool will look out of proportion.

The balance of design is as important as the delicate bal-

Planting spots can break through the informal pool's outline—varying its shape even more and enhancing its naturalistic appearance.

A modern bronze water feature brings sparkle and sounds to brighten a San Francisco garden. Water rushes over the top and splashes against the ribs of the sculpture.

ance of the homemade ecosystem. The perfect aquatic garden is so carefully fine-tuned that clear water, fish and plants co-exist in their nearly self-sufficient home. Whenever any of the elements grow beyond the pool's ability to contain them, more work is required from you. That usually means filtration systems or manual cleaning. I've learned, however, that the delight the water garden offers is so great, nearly anything is worth the trouble.

FINISHING TOUCHES

Crossing Over

During the design phase of your garden, you can plan an arched wooden bridge to span the pool, or perhaps, a small footbridge built level with the pool's edge. Bridges can be made to interrupt an existing path through the garden. You might even consider positioning your pool in order to create just such a situation. A paved path can lead to a formal bridge, perhaps in the Japanese style; or a natural path—mulched with pine needles or shredded bark—can lead to a rustic wooden bridge in the Adirondack style. A wooden bridge will be built on pylons set in concrete outside the edges of the pool. Alternatively, wooden piers are set into concrete, attach to and support the arch of the bridge at both ends. In a situation with a tiny pool, this construction would not only be unnecessary, but would also look out of place. In the small garden, the path can be replaced at the point where it crosses the water by one stone strategically placed in the pool itself; the natural gait of the walker along the path flows as he or she steps from path to stone to path. A stepping stone or footbridge level with the coping of the pool edge also provides a place to stand for maintenance or planting the pool.

Stepping stones, one, two or more, are effective and easy to place in concrete pools, but most of our pool constructions are made of plastic or rubber liner. In these cases it is a little more difficult to secure the stones, however, sure footing is a necessity and care must be taken so as not to tear the liner. Use left-over liner material to protect the pool bottom when placing stones. Place a patch of liner over an area of the pool bottom and put cinder blocks on top of the swatch. Shift them carefully until they feel secure. Flat stones can be placed on top. The blocks need never show, and they will make a solid foundation for stepping stones. You can level the top stones with bits of flat rocks used to shim the edges until they are secure. The top rocks can be cemented to the blocks, but keep in mind that this will contribute lime to the water, and the resulting rise in alkalinity must be dealt with (page 33).

My own small water garden has one long bluestone paver,

The informal pool may have a free-form outline, but it still can be placed in a spot intended for paving. At Waterford Gardens in New Jersey, irregularly shaped flat stones provide ample room for a view.

the same material as the path that spans the pool. I planned this element from the start. The pool appears to be shaped like a foot print, although, it is really more like an hourglass. The paver rests on the pinched area of the pool. Concrete, which holds the rocks along the pool edge, also supports the ends of the bridge and secures the liner. Fish swim from one side of the pool to the other. The area beneath the bridge is quite narrow, but that fact is concealed by the bridge itself.

Lighting

Because the pool is one of the most attractive parts of the garden by day, wouldn't it be wonderful to have it a highlight of the garden by night too? Until recently, the fixtures available left a lot to be desired. Most were designed for commercial uses, such as lighting a path at a sports arena, civic center or hotel, or they were simply waterproofed versions of driveway lights that were suitable for evening basketball games, but not very subtle. It's hard to create the mood of a deep and majestic lagoon with four hundred watts reflecting off of a tiny pool. Worse still, are the ubiquitous two-feet-tall "mushroom" lights —hideous eyesores by day, glowing toadstools by night. They ruin the look of every garden in which I've ever seen them.

However, in the last few years, low-voltage systems have flooded the market with light. Now you can find very discreet fixtures that can perform just about any task. Shadows can be cast on a wall with spot lights placed off to the side of a shrub. Sculpture can be bathed in a soft glow. Path lights can brighten the walk by night, and be nearly invisible by day. A small spot light can be placed at the base of a tree to illuminate its trunk and foliage. If it is next to the pool, the tree will throw a reflection from the water's surface.

Another kind of lighting of interest to us is underwater lighting. This too is low voltage; transformers reduce electrical current to only 12 volts. There is little possibility of shock if installed properly, and as all electrical equipment in the garden goes through a ground fault interrupter circuit (page 22), there is virtually no chance of an accident.

The most common underwater light looks like a small automobile headlight sealed in a plastic and rubber casing. Wires lead out from this fixture to a low-voltage transformer that plugs into a nearby outlet. The cord, of course, must be concealed with a few rocks where it comes out of the pool, where it can then be buried under soil as it leads to the outlet. The fixture can be placed on a timer designed for outdoor use.

Colored gels are available for this fixture so you can "dye" your water, red or green for example, with light. The colors can look a bit muddied when they shine through the water, though. I like the plain bulb best. Our water has plenty of color already—usually green from plants and algae. Light reflects off of the particles suspended in the water so that pool itself seems to glow.

Plants are beautiful when they are back lit. In the shallows, a bit of the light will shine through the water and up to illuminate a trickling waterfall or catch the hanging branches of a weeping shrub or arching cattail.

You will probably want to conceal the light fixture itself. The small housing is usually black and not too noticeable by itself, but if you come close to the pool at night and peer in, you will be staring at a bright, exposed bulb. Placing the fixture behind a potted waterlily or rock will solve this problem.

Despite its obvious allure, the technology of outdoor lighting could use some improvement. For me, the bulbs, which are quite expensive, burned out too quickly, and the fixture itself corroded in about a year. I have been assured that this is not the average experience. I hope that the rapid developments in the outdoor lighting industry on the whole will lead to improved products for our water gardens in the near future. Catalogs (page 89) will offer new systems as they become available.

CHOOSING THE RIGHT SPOT

Perhaps the most important aspect of designing a water garden is its placement in the landscape. If aesthetics were the only factor, this still would be a serious task, but there are many considerations that go into deciding where to locate the pool, pond or water feature. After all, installing a water garden is a big job. Moving one is next to impossible.

The choices for siting a water garden are nearly limitless. Some thoughts, however, could be considered rules for placement. Water naturally settles in the lowest part of the landscape—in nature and in your garden. So you might think the pool should be located there. You should *know* the lowest place in the landscape but not necessarily locate the water garden there, because runoff from rainstorms, often accompanied by muddy water, dirt and debris, will flow directly into the water. If you do have a low area where the pool would look natural, be sure it is not *the* lowest spot. As there is still an area lower than the pool, you will be able to drain the water to that place if emptying the pond becomes necessary. (You might want to dig up some of the soil in this lowest place in any event and incorporate lots of gravel to improve drainage.)

Water-garden catalogs say never to locate a pool in the shade. I wouldn't say "never." Just picture water in a dark spot. It would bring so much reflected light to that area. The warnings come for two reasons. One, waterlilies need sunlight, and lots of it. If you are developing a water garden specifically to grow waterlilies, place the pool where it will receive no fewer than six hours of direct sunshine for most of the summer—although eight or more hours would be better.

The major cause of shade is trees, which brings us to the other drawback about shade. Tree flowers in spring and leaves in fall will have to be removed from the pool, either by skimming or by covering the water feature for the two-week autumnal drop with netting. Bird netting, designed to keep creatures off berry plants, works perfectly. Just spread it over the pool or small pond for the duration. All the leaves will be caught, and the nearly invisible black net can be removed and carried to the compost pile where the leaves can be dumped out of it. The stored antibird netting will last forever. If leaves do drop to the bottom of the pool, they should be cleaned out with a large aquarium fish net secured to a stick, your hands or a pool vacuum. If they are allowed to stay, they may foul the water as they decompose. Trapped gasses from leaf decomposition will suffocate the fish in a cold area where ponds freeze over. Most fish do not succumb to cold, rather they die in winter from lack of oxygen; that is why we keep a hole in the ice with a pool heater (page 86) for gasses to escape.

The pond at Western Hill's Nursery in Occidental, California, is a re-created habitat for annuals, native and exotic plants, such as Iris pseudocorus, *yellow flag, the French fleur-de-lis.*

Sun and shade play by the waterside in Charles Cresson's Pennsylvania garden. Occasionally, tree leaves and blossoms may have to be skimmed off the surface of the water.

Trees present another problem. When you excavate, you will run into tree roots. Some trees, such as oaks, have deep roots that, while they may not get in the way, may suffer from lack of aeration when the soil surface is sealed with a pool. The pool can cause drainage problems for the tree's roots, too. Don't plan a water feature under a shallow-rooted tree such as a maple, as the chore of removing roots is just too much for you and the tree. It is best to consider a raised pool in this site. That is actually a pretty good idea (even under the oak). A small container, such as an oak half whiskey barrel, can make a good, small water element and, again, brings light to the shady spot.

Water attracts birds and wildlife, of course, but also visitors to the garden. A water feature will be a powerful magnet for guests and for you as well, especially if you incorporate sound —moving water. You must decide how you want to present the effect and control its power to appeal. Should the water feature be the focal point of the garden—in clear view from everywhere? Or should it be a bit hidden so that visitors have to follow the sounds to discover the pool, hiding behind a screen of flowering shrubs, for example?

The most important vista of the water garden might be the view from inside the house. Look through the major windows and consider how it would be to gaze out onto the pool. You could create a year-'round viewing garden from the picture window in the living room or perhaps the breakfast nook. The water garden will also look wonderful when the edges are covered with snow.

Reflections in the pool are about the nicest aspect of the water garden. However, when the pool is located near the house, realize that the building will be reflected in the pool from some angles. If you don't think the elevation of the house is going to look good on the water surface, this might not be the best location for the pool. The reflection can be enhanced with plants, such as shrubs that are small enough to peer over, or with small ornamental trees that you can see through to the pond.

Consider decorating the outside of the house a bit if it is to be reflected. A tree can be espaliered against the house. Espaliers are usually fruiting trees trained into fan shapes to grow flat against a wall. A flowering tree such as a *Cornus kousa*, the Asian dogwood, can also be used. Trellises can be built against the house wall and covered with flowering vines to enhance the view and its reflection. You might even attach a decorative fountain to the outside wall of the house as the source of the water to the pond. However, someday your house will need painting or other exterior servicing, and the pool should not make that impossible. A pool placed up to the wall of the house should be small, at least the edge that is shared by the house foundation. At times you could lay boards across the pool for house maintenance, if plantings would not be damaged. (Boards can be useful for servicing the pool and pruning hard-to-reach plants as well. A

The Pool Table

I created an outdoor table using a water garden as a base. I purchased a large glazed ceramic cache-pot designed as a decorative pot cover for large plants indoors. (Mine is black, but a decorated pot would be as nice if not nicer.) The top rim is about 20 inches across. I got four disks of solid, clear acrylic made of slices from a plastic rod. These are easy to buy from a plastic supplier. The disks are about a quarter inch thick and an inch in diameter. I glued them, spaced equally, around the top edge of the rim of the ceramic tub with clear silicone caulk. Then I bought a quarter-inch-thick, two-foot-diameter circle of glass—just larger than the tub—to place on top of the disks. Because the glass doesn't rest on the pot rim, it allows for air circulation and keeps out debris.

I placed some oxygen-ating plants in the water, and they seemed to keep it clean and clear. Sunlight could cause clouding from algae, so a pool in shade can be a lot easier to maintain; the water also stays cooler, and that's better for most plants and fish. I floated some water lettuce on the surface. They did not put on the spectacular show that they would in more sunlight. Nonetheless, this tub did become a brilliant, bright green oasis under the trees.

I stocked this little water feature with some eighteen-cent feeder gold-fish from the aquarium store so that if the pool attracted mosquitoes, they would be quickly gobbled up. Still—water does attract insects, but think of it as a trap and not just a lure. If you stock all your water creations, you will be reducing the mosquito population.

The serene majesty of still waters speaks of all the soothing calm that water imparts. In the shadows of Magnolia Plantations in Charleston, South Carolina, a bit of the sky is captured in reflections through tree leaves and wisteria in spring.

Sometimes a handsome duck couple may make your pool their home. Two such friends live year 'round by the formal water lily pools at the Brooklyn Botanic Garden.

Jim and Connie Cross planned for pumps, lighting, plant irrigation and other utilities before they installed their pool, which serves as foreground for another area planted with specimens from their vast collection of unusual plants.

few 2-by-6-inch boards, long enough to span the pool, will be welcome for occasional tasks.) The house will cast shade too (although, obviously, leaf drop won't be a problem there). Remember that the north side of a house is nearly always in shade. East and west sides will cast shade for half the day. The southern exposure will be in sun nearly all day in summer. One other nice thing about having a pond near the house is that water attracts birds as much as feeders do. They will come right up to the house to bathe and drink. Since there will always be a hole in the ice for gasses to escape, it will also be an opening for overwintering birds to come and drink (page 86). Being close to the house, unwanted wildlife may be more

timid about approaching the water.

If a spot next to the house acts like a wind tunnel in summer, a fountain there may not be the best idea. Water will blow away from the pool surface to paved areas around it, removing water from the pool and creating a slippery surface on paving. If it goes on long enough, algae and moss will grow on the paving—that's even more slippery and more dangerous. Wind is a consideration for siting any fountain or vertical water feature. A fountain should never be placed in a very windy area.

Be sure you know the whereabouts of underground pipes and utility lines in the vicinity of your intended site. You don't want to begin excavation and find that you are going to break

into a drainpipe or place the pool directly above the septic tank. If the pond is near the house, you will not have too many problems supplying electricity and water to service it. However, when searching through the landscape for the best place for the pool, remember that you will have to bring utilities to fill the pool and run a filter or pump. New utility lines can be buried below the soil, but consider the expense for long distances.

All outdoor electric lines must be run through a GFI or GFCI outlet (ground fault interrupter or ground fault circuit interrupter), a very sensitive plug that will shut off if any moisture enters the line. (These are usually required by codes. You've probably seen them in new bathrooms. They often have a little red light to show when they are operative.) Because water is all around the outlet for the pool, it is a necessity. Fortunately, all outlets run in sequence beyond a GFI will trip if water enters anywhere. Just think, you can safely install low-voltage underwater lighting for intriguing nighttime effects (page 17).

The GFI is reset by pushing a button. This mini circuit breaker is handy for the pool because you can easily shut off electricity to the pump for maintenance. It is impossible to get a shock from electric lines that are run properly through a GFI.

Avoid construction in especially rocky areas, which make digging so much harder. A glacier went through my backyard several thousand years ago, and I had no choice but to remove rocks. Many were saved to create the naturalistic edging around my pool. I also built a rock garden around the waterfall. Rock-garden plants grow throughout this raised area, making the waterfall, which emanates from higher ground and pours down the rocks to the pool below, look natural.

Plan access for machinery if the pool is to be large. A backhoe or bulldozer may be needed to dig the hole or move and remove rocks. Even if you'll only need to get a wheelbarrow to the location of a simple pool, be sure that it will be easy to maneuver.

A stream runs around an island planted with hardy, evergreen bamboo. It is a picture in all seasons of the year—snow in winter only enhances this water feature's beauty.

Rules and Regulations

Most communities have regulations for swimming pools. Usually pools have to be enclosed by fences three feet high to keep out little children. This is of course to prevent accidents. You might not think that this has anything to do with garden pools, and it is likely that the ordinances do not relate to pools under a certain size. However, if you have very young children, you might want to put off building a water garden for a couple of years. It is probably a good idea to check local ordinances. A shallow pool or raised tub might be a good choice when children get a little older.

INSTALLATION

You might think digging a pool is as simple as planting a shrub. Many a mail-order catalog would have you believe this. If you have access to a backhoe and bulldozer, or perfectly sifted, stone-free soil (the kind they have on those TV garden shows), you'd be home free. But few of us live in such a perfect world. Digging the hole will be work.

If you can plan for a water garden in the early days of designing the new landscape, you will save yourself many problems. However, most of us come to water gardening a little late in our green careers. If I had to do it all over again, I would create my water garden before another inch of garden was developed. I planned for the water feature as I planned my entire landscape, but I didn't get around to creating it until quite a few elements of the landscape were in place. It is much easier to excavate for a pool—or for anything, such as a tree root ball, for example, if there is plenty of space in which to work. An amorphous, free-form shape can easily be carved out in an open area of lawn. Some of you will be in this luxurious circumstance —you just dig right in. For the rest of us, it is a good idea to remove any plants from the adjacent spaces before excavation begins. These can be potted and kept watered in a holding area, a temporary nursery bed or replanted in a new home elsewhere in the landscape.

One important decision is how large the pool is to be. This requires more consideration than just appearance. How much time do you have to devote to the water garden? Larger can mean more work. Usually, the more fish, plants, gallons of water, the more maintenance. Only you know if this is pressure or pleasure. In some ways, I think larger is better. My interest outgrew my pool's size quickly. I wish I had more space for water plants and fish of every color. But if I did have a larger pool there wouldn't be much space for the flower garden, trees, shrubs, wildflowers and groundcovers that adorn my property. And there might not be enough room for the other purposes of a garden: recreation and relaxation. Today there are many devices to help in pool maintenance, such as elaborate filtration systems, so my *next* pool will probably be a larger pool.

In Helen Stoddard's magnificent water garden setting in Massachusetts, every aspect of the landscape has received the utmost attention from the skilled eye of an artist in the garden. Trees, shrubs, lawn, water, light and sound are perfectly balanced.

You've read the chapter on design and siting. Now you'll have to choose the material from which to make your pool. The options are:

- a prefab or fiberglass liner
- plastic or rubber sheeting
- a natural earth-bottom pond
- concrete or a similar material poured or sprayed over steel mesh reinforcement
- concrete block
- an aboveground container

You will most likely be excavating for a pool of manageable size and employing a liner made of a synthetic material. Rigid fiberglass liners are probably the easiest to install. Plastic film, made of polyvinyl chloride (PVC), is the least expensive. The thinnest PVC liner should last about ten years. A rubber liner is more expensive but could last up to forty years. Prefabricated rigid fiberglass can last fifty years or longer.

The fiberglass liner requires a substantial investment at the outset. Depending on size, one will cost anywhere from $150 for a small round tub holding about 50 gallons, to nearly $1,000 for a large free-form shape that contains 550 gallons. To this, add shipping, which can be substantial for the larger models, at least 20 percent above the initial cost. However, if you remember that the liner will last fifty years or longer, the initial expense isn't so hard to swallow.

The drawbacks to these liners are that there is a limit to shapes and sizes available, and none is deeper than 18 inches, the absolute minimum depth for a pool. The configurations are often described as muffin, dogbone, crescent, kidney, lamb chop, teardrop, butterfly, rectangles and circles. As interest in water gardening increases, the choices undoubtedly will grow.

The procedure for installing a rigid fiberglass liner begins with the choice of shape and size, after the site has been decided upon, following the instructions in the previous chapter. Don't locate the liner (or any pool) at the lowest part of your property. In heavy rainstorms, runoff could go beneath the liner and shift it.

When this liner arrives, place it on the desired location. Be sure to look at it from several vantage points around the property, and if you can, view it from an upstairs window or from the top of a ladder. Make adjustments to the position. This is a job for two people. You should view it and have a friend make adjustments, turning it left or right, moving it back and forth.

When you're set on the placement, assemble about six to twelve wooden stakes, depending on the size of the liner, that are taller than the fiberglass container is deep, about 30 inches tall. Push these into the ground around the liner to secure it and also create straight lines down to the soil. With a hoe, spade or similar tool, trace the liner's outline on the soil. Then remove the liner and proceed to dig the hole. Dig it about four inches wider than the outline and at least two inches deeper.

As you dig down, you might be surprised at some of the things you unearth: old bottles, tin cans, car fenders. . . . Set aside all large rocks for possible use around the liner's edge. Make the sides of the hole as smooth as possible. Make sure no sharp stones protrude beyond the sides. Pour and spread sand over the bottom of the hole to aid in leveling and positioning the liner. The top edge should end up being slightly higher than the surrounding ground. It must be level. Nothing looks worse than if the water in the pool is

---

How Many Gallons are in Your Pool?

For many tasks, such as choosing a filter or treating the fish with medicine, you have to know how many gallons are in your pool. This isn't too hard if you have a square pool or if you had a water meter when you filled the pool for the first time. However, there are formulas to determine the volume of a pool.

For a rectangle, start with a formula for determining cubic feet: length × width × depth = number of cubic feet. One cubic foot contains 7.5 gallons of water. So a pool 5 feet by 10 feet by 2 feet deep holds 100 cubic feet. 100 cubic feet × 7.5 = 750 gallons of water.

For a circular pool: 3.14 × (½ the diameter × ½ the diameter) × depth = cubic feet × 7.5 = gallons.

An oval or oblong pool: length × width × depth × 6.7 = gallons.

Irregular, free-form pools: Often, pool size has to be approximated because of irregularly shaped designs. Try to combine shapes to make the pool into circles, an oval or general rectangle. Estimate the general size and shape and round off the results. My pool is shaped like a giant footprint. For purposes of calculating water volume, this shape could be considered a circle plus an oval.

uneven so that some of the liner's side is exposed and the other is at water level.

Use a large carpenter's or mason's level to make sure the pool is even and fill with sand under one end of the bottom or remove some from the other to adjust it. There is a new, inexpensive level available, simply a clear plastic hose with two lines marked on it. When water in the hose touches both lines, they are level. One end of the tube can be held against one part of the liner's edge, the other against another. Obviously, you'll need your friend's help for this, too. The liner may have to be removed a few times and reset.

When the liner is level (and just above the elevation of the surrounding soil), begin to fill it with water. As you do, back fill the sides of the hole with the excavated soil, making sure that you get soil all around the liner and down to the bottom. If you sift the soil through hardware cloth before you pour it into the surrounding space, rocks and debris will be removed and it will be easier to push into place; also, no sharp objects will come in contact with the liner. Use a broomstick or rake handle to prod the soil into place. Continue to add water and soil until you have brought both up to the original level of the soil. When you have finished bringing up the soil line, run the hose around the filled edge and add more soil if necessary. As with all in-ground pools, you will want to conceal the edge of the liner to enhance its appearance with some type of edging. The most formal, of course, is to surround it with

uniformly cut stone pavers, such as flagstone.

There is a great impulse to have lawn go right to the edge of the liner. With a rigid liner, this is possible. If you don't mind the look of the slightly exposed fiberglass edge, you could conceivably have lawn touch the liner. Maintenance will be a bit difficult; you could be able to use a string trimmer (a weed whacker), or you might have to use a scissors-type hand trimmer. Of course, if you want to have marsh plants grow right to the edge, then plan to leave spaces to install these plants.

A naturalistic, soillike edging can be made from a "pudding" of clean garden loam and cement. Mix five parts soil to one part cement, and if needed, add water to make a consistency that can be patted into place. This edging should look like a gentle mound of soil around the edge of the pool. Leave planting pockets open for moisture-lovers to grow right up to the pool edge. Keep this amalgam moist by covering it with plastic for at least three days. If any cement mixture gets into the water, or any soil or debris from construction, you will have to drain the pool and refill it. Brush the edge with vinegar when it has dried. Soil can be filled up to this pudding edging.

You can also use some of the rocks that you removed to create a rocky setting for the pool or even a rock garden. Some of the rocks can be cemented together —you can even set them in the soil-cement mixture. You can also install a waterfall at one end. One thing to keep in mind

The water feature at the new Atlanta Botanical Garden presents a simple line of coping to meet the edge of grass lawn. This strip also facilitates cutting— the mower's wheel simply glides along the flat pavers.

is that the water for the falls should seem to emanate from the most logical point—the place where an imaginary stream would enter the waterfall flow, and spill into the garden pool.

Flexible plastic liners made of PVC are the least expensive materials to use to make a pool. The process is similar to that for the fiberglass liner. The major difference is that you can create nearly any shape you want. Of course, from a design point, it's great to be able to customize the pool; however, you

The undulating border of the informal pool subdues the evidence of its master's hand by presenting opportunities to grow plants right up to the water and soften its rigid edge.

Drainpipes and Overflows

A drawback to these liners is that it is very hard to add a drain or an overflow tube. These would have to be constructed by putting a hole in the liner bottom and fitting a drain or a pipe through the hole. It is helpful to have the option of draining the pool for cleaning, and to be able to get some of the water out of the pool in heavy rainstorms. Unfortunately, punching holes in the liner is too destructive in most cases.

You might consider making a small indenta-tion in the edging so that water can overflow there; you'll have to pre-pare for overflow by back-filling this place with lots of gravel. This can cause problems if the area out-side the liner becomes so soggy that things start to shift.

After heavy rainstorms, I bale the water with buckets, and that might be the best solution. However, it is not always easy to find a place in the garden to pour the wa-ter when everything is already saturated.

will ultimately have to make the liner conform to the excavation's space and shape. That is not as easy as you might think. The catalogs would have you imag-ine that you dig a hole, lay a liner over it, fill the liner with water and watch it sink per-fectly into place. The liner will actually have to be cajoled into place and the edges carefully pleated and folded. Again, this is not a job for one person. You must bury and disguise the ends of the plastic sheeting, not just to make it more attractive, to hide the area where you bury the liner's edge, but also to se-cure it permanently.

To determine the liner size measure the length and width of the anticipated pool at its widest point. You'll want this pool to be at least 24 inches deep at the lowest point. If your pool *is* to be 2 feet deep, you'll have to add at least 4 feet to the liner's width and length. You should also add one foot on all sides to have enough liner edge to bury to hold it in position. Therefore, liner length equals length + 2 × pool depth + 2 feet for liner edge. Liner width equals pool width dimension + 2 × pool depth + 2 feet for liner edge. This will work for any shape pool, even free form.

A small PVC liner of the thin-nest gauge (20 millimeters), one for a half whiskey barrel, for instance, about 5 feet wide by 5 feet long, would cost about $25. The largest liner of this gauge you might be able to find is approximately 30 feet by 30 feet. This liner would cost about $600. It could be used for a pool approximately 26 feet square and 18 inches deep. It would hold nearly *8,000* gallons. This is a good-size pool for a home garden. Custom-made liners are available for larger pools. This gauge of liner should last at least ten years, especially if no part of the liner is directly ex-posed to sunlight. PVC is bro-ken down by ultraviolet rays.

Other liner material choices include heavier gauges of PVC, 32 millimeters, for example, which should last fifteen to twenty years. These liners come in a few colors. Years ago, they only came in "swimming-pool" blue—an impossible color for a natural-looking pool. Try to get the darkest color, which is of-ten dark gray.

The longest-lasting flexible liners are made of 45-millimeter rubber. This is often called Bu-tyl rubber, a synthetic product. This liner is black. You might expect a black liner to heat the water, but usually it becomes covered with a thin layer of algae soon after installation, which not only reduces the light- and heat-absorption properties but also makes it look quite natural. These liners produce a very realistic, deep appearance and last thirty years or longer. The 30- by 30-foot sheet compares well at a cost of about $1,000.

You have to be extremely careful when you prepare the hole for the flexible liner so that no sharp objects, not even stones, protrude beyond the soil. The bottom of the hole must be covered, and to be extra cautious, even the sides. Some people use damp newspaper for this. I've even heard of using old carpeting. Some suppliers now offer a thick fabric for this purpose through catalogs as well. In most situations, when sharp stones are few and easily removed, sand in the bottom of the hole will do.

PREPARING THE HOLE FOR A PLASTIC LINER

Draw the design of the pool in the landscape. You can use a length of garden hose for this purpose. Move the hose around to outline different shapes until you create one that is pleasing. Be sure to view this shape from all parts of the landscape and from house windows—upstairs, too, if possible. Some naturalistic shapes include the familiar kidney, and a rough hour-glass shape (one that later could be spanned by a walkway or moon bridge, a bridge in the Japanese style that forms a gentle arch over the water). You can draw the outline directly on the soil or grass by pouring a bit of powdered hydrated lime, sold at garden centers, from a coffee can or bag.

Start to remove the soil in the area. Remember to create shelves for marginal or marsh plants in containers. These can be made on one side of the pool hole or all around the edge. The shelf should hold container plants with their pot rims at the suggested level beneath the water; this is often about 3 inches. If you estimate a pot to be about 8 inches tall, then the shelf could be made about 12 inches below the liner's edge, and it should be 10 to 12 inches wide for the container to sit securely. (Larger plants can be placed directly in the pool and elevated on inverted pots or bricks, so they are brought up to the appropriate height.)

Start digging from the outside edge and create the shelf areas. Sculpt all sides to pitch slightly toward the center of the pool so that you are making a kind of pie plate—about a 75-degree angle. Head toward the center area of the pool. The ultimate depth of the pool should be at least 24 inches. You will be adding sand or another soft

Make It Level

Place a level, spirit level on a line, or the clear plastic hose level described on page 27 across the excavation. If you don't have one long enough to reach, you can make a fair substitute. Tape a small level to the thin edge of a 2- by 4-inch piece of lumber long enough to cross your pool at the widest point. Make sure you select a piece of lumber that is very straight. You can judge this by "eye-balling" the lumber: Hold one end and peer down the length to see if it bows or twists. Lay the board on its narrow side on a surface that you know to be level, perhaps the floor of the garage (check it with the small carpenter's level). Check the board with the level to see how flat it is. Tape the level to the top, the 2-inch end, so that the wood will not bow when placed across the opening. If necessary, you can pitch the carpenter's level with a wooden shim to adjust for any imperfection in the board.

You can also make your own plastic hose level. Purchase a length of clear vinyl hose, at least a half inch inside diameter, and at least 10 feet long from an aquarium supply store, plastic supplier or even a large hardware store. Place a piece of masking tape around the tubes about 6 inches from both ends. Fill the tube with water so that the liquid touches both pieces of tape.

material to protect the liner from stones or other things that might puncture it from below, so excavate at least another 2 inches down to accommodate this cover. Try to plan for a slope in the bottom of the pool as well. This is so that in the event a pump has to be used to empty the pond, water will go to the lowest part. Pond debris will also drift to this area, making cleaning easier, as well.

Move the leveling board around the hole as you work. Measure a length of wood that is as long as the pool will be deep. Check the depth around the pool bottom by holding the wood up to the bottom edge of a 2-by-4 laid across the top of the hole. This will keep your depth consistent.

When you've finished digging for the pool, cut an extra ledge beyond the hole's sides, a foot wide and about an inch deep,

for concealing the liner. The liner's border may end up being laid in this area and covered with coping, flat stone or brick curbing, to disguise it. In most cases, the stone coping should extend a little bit over the water to conceal the edge of the liner and create the illusion that the water flows beneath the stones. If you plan to make this paving permanent, that is, make it possible for visitors to actually walk along the paved edge of the pool, the ledge must be deeper because you will have to prepare a solid base for the stones. You'll find instructions for finishing the liner's edge on page 31.

After the hole is completely prepared, stretch the entire liner over the hole and center it. Weight the four corners with bags of sand or heavy stones set on several layers of folded newspaper. Place a garden hose

into the center of the stretched liner and start to fill it with water. As it fills, the weight of the water will make the liner sink slowly into the hole and it will conform approximately to its shape. The weights keep it taut and they will slide along the ground with the liner. When the pool is nearly filled, you'll have to smooth the sides as best as you can. It is impossible to get them to conform completely. You will have to fold and pleat portions of the material. Unfortunately, cold water adds to the difficulty by stiffening the plastic. The liner won't look great at this stage, but remember that you will be burying the top edge and covering the rim with rocks or other edging materials. Water and plants will also hide a lot of the imperfections. Do not give up at this stage!

When you are sure that the liner is completely in place,

Plants for the water garden are potted in containers and sunk to the appropriate depth for the individual (see Plant Portraits page 57). This includes marginal plants such as iris, left, and the waterlily to its right. An excavated shelf for the marginal plants, which surrounds the pool's inside edge, is planned from the beginning. Rocks disguise and hold the pool's liner in place (far left and far right).

carefully trim the excess with sharp scissors. Be sure to leave at least 12 inches beyond the rim of the pool. The liner edge can be buried in a trench dug about 6 inches beyond the rim and about 6 inches deep. If you are going to make a neat coped edge of rocks, they can be placed directly over the plastic edge—recessed about one inch deep. You can, however, tack the edges of the liner with 10-inch nails in a few places to keep it in place as you work.

If your choice for the edging is flagstone, slate or other quarried stone, consider taking an accurate scale drawing of the pool to the stone supplier to help with your purchase. You'll have to play around with the stones until they "fit." When you have arranged them to your liking, number all the stones with chalk. Try to write the numbers so that they all point in the same direction so you will not only have their position recorded but also their orientation. If you want to set the stones in mortar to create a stationary edging, then you will have to excavate an extra 3 inches to compensate for a wet mortar base for the stones (the ledge will have to be deeper). If you intend to walk on this edging, then the footing of concrete will have to be even thicker, especially in cold climates where freezing and thawing may cause stones in shallower mortar to heave. Paving such as this could be set on a 12-inch-deep footing of concrete, so that an extra-deep trench next to the pool will have to be prepared. This may be a job for a professional.

At least get advice from the stone yard on preparing this footing for pavers set in mortar.

If you use any concrete around the pool, remember that it is very alkaline. Not only will you have to wear gloves to keep from burning your hands but you will also have to empty the pool and refill it because the water will be too alkaline for fish and plants. And concrete, either from the edging or from the construction of a waterfall, will have to be cured using vinegar. You could invest in an inexpensive water pH-testing kit to make sure that the water is near neutral—not too acid, not too alkaline—for fish and plants. Chemicals are available to adjust the pH of the water once you have refilled the pool. (Water will also have to be treated for chlorine and chloramine. More on this on page 54.)

If there's enough room on your property for a large earth-bottom pond, this might be for you. It is not a job that you can do yourself. Often a natural pond is dug to interrupt the course of a stream. The stream will have to be diverted during the process. The idea is to make a huge bulge in the stream's path, something that will look a bit like the boa constrictor that swallowed an elephant.

In many communities, even in rural areas, officials will have something to say about this procedure. It is a rare situation when a stream begins and ends on the same property. The stream probably travels a distance through many properties, and the diversion and ultimate pooling of the stream may affect neighbors. You may have to get

Flagstone was the choice for pavement around this naturalistic swimming pool. Extending the pavers over the edge makes it seem as if the water flows under the stone and softens the hardness of this immutable material.

The professional installation of a waterfall and pool by Long Island's Rockwater, Inc., uses rocks and stones of many sizes in combinations. The painstaking arrangement and rearrangement of rocks is remarkable.

If you are blessed with moving water on your property, such as a stream, you can define its edge with stones and enliven it with plants selected to blend in with the setting.

a permit to do this job. You never want to stop a stream; just slow it down for a bit. Check with local officials, your county extension service or ask pond makers about restrictions and permits.

In some areas, you can find people who dig ponds listed in the telephone book. Your local "ag" store (agricultural supply), nursery/garden center or county extension service agent will probably know who digs ponds in your area. This should not be too expensive. Professionals should know how to do this job, but some of the responsibility

is up to you. Ask to see examples of their work. And make sure the schedule for completion is in the contract, with reference to weather contingencies. Professionals should be willing to accept responsibility if something goes wrong, for example, if the water table of your property, the natural level of water in the ground, will conflict with the pond's development.

The earth-bottomed pond is dug to the desired depth and as wide and long as you want. Sometimes the soil at the bottom of the hole is mostly clay—a nearly waterproof medium. This clay could be pounded with tools or machinery to pack it down and make it even more watertight. If the hole does not have natural clay, clay can be brought in by the truckload. If the pond is to be built in a sandy location, a large rubber liner (page 27) will have to be set in place, and your pond won't be earth-bottomed after all.

Concrete garden pools have virtually been replaced by plastic-liner pools. However, in warm climates and in the case of formal pools, concrete is still utilized. Concrete is a mixture of Portland cement and sand or gravel. Often, three parts sand are mixed with one part cement and enough water to make a thick but not stiff amalgam. Once the concrete has set, it is very strong; nevertheless, it may crack in cold climates from moisture expanding as it becomes ice. If it is properly prepared, not too wet, not too dry, reinforced correctly and allowed to set slowly, it should not be affected by freezing and thawing.

The concrete pond is more expensive than the liner and much more work to install. You would be well advised to hire a professional to do the work. In any event, here's an idea of how it's done. Half-inch tie rods or #3 construction wire, or both, have to be incorporated into the concrete. The rods can also be fashioned into an 8-inch grid and connected with wire ties. The walls should be made to slope outward slightly. This will help the material stay in place as it is applied, and later make cleaning and draining more efficient. The walls and floor of the concrete pool are made at least 6 inches thick. You will not need a casting form for the mixture if it is firm enough to trowel into place. Push it through the mesh and down from the outside, and then work toward the waterside—on the inside of the mesh. (Remember, this is very much like putting in a swimming pool. Today, even swimming pools are being made with plastic liners. When concrete or concretelike materials are used, they are often sprayed onto wire frames.)

The concrete can be installed in layers but the bottom and sides should meet in one "pouring" if possible. And all of the work should be done in one day, best if it is cool and overcast. The idea is for the concrete to dry as slowly as possible. In heat and sun, it would dry too quickly. However, the temperature should not be below 50 degrees Fahrenheit, and it should not be raining.

Cement hardens by means of a chemical reaction not unlike

that of plaster of Paris. The hardening does not come from drying but from the heat that occurs as a reaction to water, the catalyst. After the concrete is poured, it must remain damp until the material has set. Sprinkle with water after pouring and make sure it stays damp. Masons used to cover the material with burlap or other fabric soaked in water and replace it as it began to dry, for days, even weeks. Today we have clear plastic film (polyethylene) that will help keep the material wet if it is placed around the bottom and sides and carefully sealed. An advantage to clear plastic is that you can see the condensation through the film and check moisture that way. A disadvantage is that sunlight passes through the material and can make the concrete dry out if it is not properly sealed. You might want to use a combination of wet rags and plastic. As soon as the concrete is strong enough, the pool can be filled with water. This will keep it wet as it continues to strengthen.

Again, cement is extremely alkaline, so much so that it can create a similar reaction as pure acid would, burning humans, fish and plants. The concrete must be cured to neutralize the "free lime" in the water. Household vinegar works well. It is safe to use, readily available and inexpensive. Mix 1 gallon of vinegar to every 200 gallons of pool water. Let the pool stand for at least three days, then drain it completely, hose it down and fill it with water again, this time for fish and plants. Check pH before stocking the pool.

You may also choose to paint on a special pool sealer—a rubberized, nontoxic paint for this purpose. Although concrete is quite attractive under water—it looks blue—it can become permanently stained.

There are a few advantages to concrete. You can easily install a drain without the puncture problem of a plastic liner. You can also have a strainer built into the construction, just as is done for swimming pools. The strainer skims debris off the top of the water and pours it through a mesh basket that can be emptied. The greatest advantage of all is that a properly reinforced and poured concrete pool will outlast all the other materials.

Concrete blocks (cinder blocks) can be used below ground to build walls for a pool. Here again, you might want to call in a professional. A deep hole is dug to about 6 or 8 inches deeper than the pool will ultimately be—24 to 30 inches deep. The hole is lined with about 2 inches of gravel. Steel rods are driven into the soil around the perimeter. The rods can be used to anchor construction wire, which spans the entire excavation and rests 2 to 3 inches above the gravel floor. You'll need either to have concrete from a cement mixer delivered to the site at the appropriate time or rent a portable mixer, for you will need quite a bit of this material. Concrete is poured into the hole to a thickness of about 6 inches. (Eventually, hosed-down blocks will be threaded down the rods. The blocks will also be filled

If concrete is used to cement rocks in place for a waterfall or pool step, steps must be taken to test and neutralize the alkalinity of this material. Vinegar can be used, but it's best to check the pH with a small kit sold by water-garden suppliers.

with more concrete after they are mortared in place.)

This kind of construction will have to be cured just as the poured concrete pool is. And in both situations, a coating might also be desirable. Any nontoxic, waterproof paint can be used, but rubber-based paints are ideal for this use. They are sold by the water-garden catalogs specifically for coating concrete.

Stone walls form the sides of this above-ground pool in Atlanta, Georgia. At the rear of the pool, water constantly pours over a large ball finial recycled as garden sculpture.

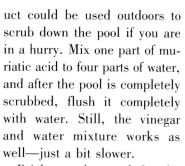

If you want to create an above-ground container for a water garden, then reinforced concrete or concrete block are choices, often used for large formal fountains. In the case of reinforced concrete, a form is built, most often from wood, and iron rods are pounded inside the frame and into the ground. Wire mesh may also be placed inside the frame and attached to the rods. The pool is excavated so that the bottom is below ground level. The flat bottom has to be reinforced with wire mesh as with all the concrete pools.

These containers have to be cured. And they must also be etched in order for paint or coating to adhere to the blocks of concrete. In these cases, the outside of the constructions may be painted as well as the inside. While muriatic acid is still on the market, this somewhat dangerous and very toxic prod-

uct could be used outdoors to scrub down the pool if you are in a hurry. Mix one part of muriatic acid to four parts of water, and after the pool is completely scrubbed, flush it completely with water. Still, the vinegar and water mixture works as well—just a bit slower.

Brick can be used for the walls too, but you would have to use several thicknesses, three or more, to support the pressure of the water on the inside of the construction. Brick containers can also be designed to hold a PVC liner. They could be used as a round or square wall which becomes a frame for a plastic liner, which might not need a concrete pad at the bottom for support. The brick wall, however, will require subterranean concrete piers for support.

Another way to create an aboveground pool would be to use a fiberglass liner surrounded by concrete block, with concrete poured between the mortared blocks and the water-filled liner. You may also find some premade fountains. These come in formal shapes and often in several sections to be cemented together with mortar. There are many variations in shape. However, these are very expensive. Most of them are imported and made to resemble stone. Check the listing on page 89 for sources.

Concrete pools and concrete block pools will need some special winter care. It's best if the pools can be drained. There are also floating devices that compress if ice forms, to absorb the pressure of the expanding ice. Often heaters are used to keep holes in ice for the health of the fish. This hole

The formal pool at Old Westbury Gardens in Old Westbury, New York, is made with concrete set into the ground. It is designed as much to be viewed from a great distance as close up.

will absorb the force of the pushing ice as well.

A simple aboveground pool can be made, as mentioned before, from small containers such as half whiskey barrels, whether lined with plastic, painted or even left as they come. Once filled, the wood swells and makes them completely water-tight. There are also some small plastic containers that will hold up to fifty gallons without having to be reinforced. Some companies, such as Terracast™, make PVC containers in molds that are the same as those used for terra-cotta pots. These containers may be purchased without drainage holes. They cost about the same as real terra-cotta but will last for years and don't have to be brought to a frost-free location for the winter. Still, it is probably a good idea *not* to leave them filled with water over the winter. Empty them, storing the plants as described in Chapter 5, and the wildlife in indoor aquaria or larger pools outdoors.

DEFYING GRAVITY

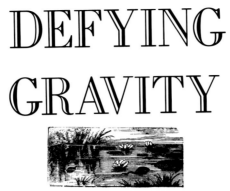

Nothing brings more magic to the garden than moving water, and this is especially true when, with your help, water defies gravity, moving uphill to cascade down a waterfall or spraying straight up into the air through a fountain. Having moving water in the garden may not be essential, but it certainly is a delightful, and to me an irresistible, aspect of water gardening. Movement also aerates the water, required by hardy, cold-water fish, especially helpful in warm weather when water holds less oxygen. Many pools or small ponds will require filtration devices of some type, in any event. Pumps and moving water are necessary for these and simultaneously available for water features. The filter not only keeps water clean for aesthetic reasons, it also is better for the health of fish.

Here again, scale is important. The moving-water feature must be balanced with the garden and pool. A torrent of gushing water might be too much from an artistic standpoint, but even a little too much water can pose a problem. Waterlilies rot if their foliage is wet for long periods, so these plants and a splashing fountain are not compatible.

There are two basic forms for moving water, which can be considered informal and formal: the waterfall and the fountain. I think waterfalls should look as natural as possible. A modern design with geometric basins overflowing from one to the next can be welcome for a formal, geometric pool, but I would categorize this as sculpture, or actually, a sculptural fountain. When I picture a waterfall, I think of glistening stones with water pouring between and over the rocks in spills and splashes—all planted with wonderful marginal plants.

The formal pool and a fountain go together just as a waterfall and informal pools do. There are mechanical things to consider: pumps, filters, pipes, spray jets, liners and the like. Fountains can be constructed and jets purchased to create nearly any configuration desired. In a large pond, a single jet can be attached to a floating, anchored fountain that sends water ten or twenty feet in the air. This fountain would be wonderful on a large property to view from a distance. On the other hand, a little pump can be concealed in a vessel that will simply produce a gurgle that just breaks the surface of the water and produces a little bit of sound.

The "white noise" produced by moving water—especially if the water is broken into tiny droplets, a kind of foamy, frothy sound—is not only delightful in the garden but it will actually cover a lot of peripheral noise. For example, this small sound can drown out quite a bit of traffic noise if the garden is located near an active street or highway. This will also enhance the feeling of privacy in a crowded urban area where town-house gardens grow right next to each other.

Catalogs of pumps and fountains explain in detail what you would need to achieve the desired effect. In general, the power of the pump

In a landscape designed by Alice Ireys, a realistic waterfall is heavily planted as it would be in nature, but here with ornamental plants such as astilbe and hardy orchid (Bletilla striata).

to move water diminishes the more the pump is required to defy gravity. In other words, if a pump can push 100 gallons of water one foot into the air every hour, then it may only be able to push 75 gallons per hour two feet into the air. The width of the spray will be determined by the shape of the opening and number of holes in the spray head, as well as the number of jets in the fountain chosen. All of these will determine the power, size and cost of the pump required. The height of a waterfall is similarly considered when buying a pump. You'll have to know how much water is needed

to produce the volume of water you want to cascade over the edge of the falls. You can test the waterfall with a garden hose. (Time how long the hose takes to fill a 5- or 10-gallon container.)

A good location for a fountain pump is directly under the fountain, limiting the distance against which the pump has to work. The piping for a waterfall will have to be planned from the outset of the pool's design, as it will have to be hidden. This pipe and the electric cord leading to the outlet also have to be concealed from view. Add a filter to the intake of the submerged pump, and you can see how complex this can become. The pump for the waterfall could be located beneath a ledge that is formed by the fall itself. The filter, too, has to be concealed if it is an in- or out-of-water type.

In olden days, this earth-defying act was accomplished by diverting mountain water via aqueducts and the like and, later, by water-wheel-driven pumps. Today's electrical pumps, although small, deliver extraor-

dinary power. In fact, when I wanted a pump to move a little bit of water gently, I was hard-pressed to find one. About the smallest pump you can find will move around fifty gallons an hour.

Most of the pumps available today are underwater devices. Set into the pool, they collect water at the inlet and push it out the other end. Many of them are attached to filters—either strainers just to keep large debris from clogging the mechanism, or substantial filters that will clean the pool's water and provide the necessary moving water to operate a waterfall or fountain. These pumps can't be set at the lowest point in the pool, however, for in the event that water from the outlet somehow gets rerouted and spills away from the pool, it is important that the pump will not be able to completely empty the pond. The reason is obvious: Fish and plants would die if all the water was removed. Pumps also must not be allowed to run dry; their motors will burn out.

To get ideas for moving water, observe wild water as well as water that has been tamed, as in this setting next to a garden made in the foundation of an old mill.

FOUNTAINS: THE FORMAL WATER FEATURES

Often an electrical pump can be used to power a fountain. The fountain defies gravity in the most visually obvious fashion. There can be a single jet of water heading skyward above a small pool or basin. This jet can reach from one foot or so to thirty feet in the air. You may

have seen fountain jets set in ponds and lakes, an old and intensely romantic convention. There are now floating devices that contain jets that are easy to place in large ponds for this effect. The water crashing back to the pond surface makes ripples, splashes and sound—lots of sound—wonderful "water music." This sound also tells the birds where to come to find the life-giving water they love.

The concept of the single jet can be extrapolated to include any manner of water display that can be created by a fitting attached to the pipe outlet from a pond. A ring of small openings will make a circle of dancing sprays. Nozzles are available to create nearly any pattern desired. You will have to make a secure base to hold the pipe and nozzle in place. You will also have to consider the location of the fountain. Wind is the problem; if the water sprays up in a windy location, the falling water will miss the pool, which will eventually run dry.

The sprays can also be made to present tiers of water splashing at different heights. Jets can make patterns described as mushrooms, for example, in which the water is broken into a domed sheet of water. There is also a dandelion effect produced by many domed or mushroom sprays arranged around a ball of jets.

A gusher delivers a great quantity of water at one time. This could be mounted on top of an urn or birdbath-type sculpture so that the water bounces, splashes and runs over the structure. Sculptures can also be piped. You have probably seen animal sculptures such as frogs

or swans spitting water into pools and troughs. These used to be made of lead, and some still are, but there are fiberglass copies made today that are much lighter and cheaper to produce and transport. Abstract constructions can be as effective. Concrete sculptures can be piped in this way too.

Some people, rather than using recycled water to power the fountain, merely hook the pipes directly up to the hose and water supply. Even in areas of abundant water, this waste can't be tolerated. Population pressure on water supplies will eventually be felt everywhere, so why not plan to have water recirculate from the start.

Water-garden supply catalogs will provide all the information necessary for determining the size and power of the pump needed for fountains. The pump will be rated as to the amount of water it can raise to a certain height per hour. For example, a pump that can lift 100 gallons per hour one foot into the air will cost about $50 and use 30 watts of electricity. A pump that can lift 4,200 gallons per hour five feet into the air will use 1100 watts and cost about $450. When you buy a pump for your fountain, you'll have to consider rate. (My pump delivers about 400 gallons per hour four feet up to the top of my waterfall.)

A decidedly formal, even unnatural waterfall becomes a water-garden sculpture beside a pool designed by New Jersey landscape architect William John Wallis, ASLA.

Where does the water come from? That question isn't even asked when the point of entry to the informal waterfall is obscured from view. The water's existence is just taken for granted by the viewer.

THE INFORMAL WATERFALL

One of the most important things to consider when thinking about creating a waterfall is where the most natural place to simulate an inlet is. If the topography of your site has high and low levels, this is simple because, naturally, water flows downhill, so you would develop the waterfall on high ground. If your pool is on a flat ground, you will want to develop a raised area; this should appear as if it is the termination of a natural stream that flows into the pool. If you are very adventuresome, you might actually develop part of the faux stream as well. Water could be pumped up to an area a ways away from the pool, and all the ground could be raised above pool level. A way to ensure the illusion of a watercourse, might be to create a "bend" in the stream. The water could come from around a corner and lead to the waterfall. Perhaps a rock outcropping could be built up some distance from the pool and water could wind around this rock. It will appear that the water comes from a distance away and turns at the rock, heading for the waterfall, but in actuality it emanates just behind the rock.

Observe a real waterfall to get ideas. Notice how water in the wild tends to pool at different heights and then overflow one raised place to fill another depression made of rock on the slope, fills that up and spills into the next level, ultimately emptying into the pool. These are like layered terraces. Sometimes water just flows over rocks on an incline and into the natural basin or stream below. This kind of construction would be harder to control; water would splash all over the rocks and some would escape the course. It is very important that your falls don't take water away. You will be constantly topping off the pool, and won't dare go on vacation for even a few days.

If you can find a stream, follow it to see how it forms little pools and falls whenever its path is obstructed by pebbles, rocks or even a fallen tree. Take snapshots if you can to help you as references for your waterfall's design. In your garden, you may want to have more than one level falling above the pool. Two, three or more layers of falling water can be spectacular. Try to imagine what the source of the water in your garden would be if there wasn't a pump. Try to make a waterfall that doesn't look as though it is springing from nowhere. Curve the waterfall a bit, or stagger its course. Conceal the filling point behind a rock, as described, or a few evergreen shrubs so that it is not clear where it comes from, but rather the water seems to start just out of view beyond those rocks where the stream runs.

For this reason and others, small prefabricated waterfalls are about as natural looking in gardens as plaster gnomes and toadstools. Preformed fiberglass waterfalls are available. These have several basins set at different heights to catch water and allow it to cascade. They can be dressed up with loose rocks, but, I must admit, I have never seen one that looks acceptably realistic. Perhaps in the future, preformed watercourses will be made that have the right scale and proportion to look indigenous to the landscape.

In the best situation, the wa-

Wind the path of the water as it splashes down the levels of the fall. In nature, the shifting landscape, rocks, fallen trees and even animals make a straight line impossible.

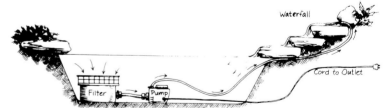

A typical garden pool waterfall uses a recirculating pump. The pump draws water in one end and delivers it to the top of the waterfall where it pours down to the pool again. A filter can be attached to the intake end of the pump to clean the water. Both the hose from the pump to the waterfall and the pump's electric cord have to come up and out of the pool or pond, not piercing the liner, and be concealed by rocks or buried in soil.

terfall is made before the pool is finished and stocked. It can be quite difficult to add one when the pool is established, as it will have to be made watertight, just like the pool. If you are siting the pool next to elevated ground or if you plan to build up one side of the pool using the material excavated from the hole, you will have the makings of a "naturally" sloping waterfall. Watercourses tend to cut through raised areas such as hills. You can carve out two or three depressions in the hill. Water will eventually be piped to fill the first basin, spill over the edge to the next one and eventually fall back to the pool. The area should be lined with plastic, either a PVC or rubber liner, and then that will be concealed by carefully selected rocks. Not only do the rocks enhance the appearance of the fall, they also add twirling movement to the water and, often, sound.

The elevated form can also be built of concrete block and mortar (or thin concrete over wire frames in climates where hard freezes are rare). The design is similar, only the levels will have to be built by varying heights of layered blocks. When you design the waterfall, consider many of the same things you did when planning the pool itself. Add planting pockets for special plants that will not only conceal the edges of the construction but also make the waterfall look pretty and more natural. Again, return to the models—the natural pool, pond and stream.

My waterfall is made of rocks that have been cemented to-

gether. To achieve the height, I first built up the layers with concrete block. I arranged rocks for the side of the falls and special rocks that I thought would be good for the spillways. I moved the rocks several times and occasionally tested the arrangement with a garden hose. I numbered all the rocks with chalk and drew arrows on them to show the direction in which they laid. I also took snapshots of the precemented arrangement. I must admit that with all of these steps there was still a bit of rearrangement when it came time to set the stones permanently in place. When finished, I brought in soil to build up the sides of the elevated waterfall and for plants. I also put some extra rocks in the soil to make the arrangement even more naturalistic.

Building a receptacle at every level of the waterfall will also help create the most dramatic effect with the least amount of water. If a trickle flows over rocks, it will just appear to add a gloss to their surfaces—nice, but not as dramatic as elevated pools that fill to the brim and then spill from some height into the level below. To heighten the splash and drama of the water falling from the elevated hollows, consider making an overhanging lip on the front edge of the rims of the waterfalls so that the water doesn't just splash onto the rocks below but has a clear drop, perhaps as a sheet of water. The rock ledges you create should be quite horizontal, and can be made of more than one rock. But any front ledge that is off kilter will look unnatural and disturbing.

The inspiration for this massive fall was nature itself. It is not revealed all at once. One must walk through woodland to find it. And yet, its presence is announced from far away by its thundering sound.

The placement of rocks for the falls will require many adjustments to get it "just right." When you think you've just about got it, use a garden hose to test the construction. Planting has just begun by this new waterfall.

In time, mosses and other plants will cover rocks and obscure edges, making the "newness" of the construction meld with its surroundings. Tucking small ferns and sections of moss in the soil around the rocks can hasten the process.

Rocks placed in the path of the water will add interest to movement. The water will swirl around the obstructions —speeding up in some spots, slowing down in others.

The Little Things

There are places around the landscape where small garden features would bring so much. If you have only a small garden, the addition of a water feature is a must. Picture that spot with the simplest water garden: a half whiskey barrel containing one miniature waterlily. Any watertight container could be used. In a similar spot, a self-contained wall fountain with a pump that recirculates water would produce sound and movement. Some such devices have built-in ornamental basins that hold as little as two gallons. A small roof terrace I know in Manhattan has a commercially available fountain secured to a brick chimney that forms part of the east wall of the elevated garden. The decorative fountain features a relief sculpture of a lion's head. The lion is piped so water pours out of its mouth and into a fluted shell-shaped bowl.

Soon I will be installing a large concrete urn in the tiniest, most ignored spot in my garden where no one ventures . . . yet. The urn will be elevated above a fiberglass con-tainer sunk into the ground surrounded by the same bluestone paving material that already covers the adjacent area. The urn will rest on a few bricks. A pump will be concealed below the urn. The drainage hole in the concrete urn will be fitted with a threaded pipe plumbing seal. Water will be drawn up from the fiberglass pan, piped up to fill and perpetually overflow the urn—rolling gently over its rim. Constantly wet, the urn will quickly "age," covered with deep green moss.

A terra-cotta jar could be used as well. These are more common and less expensive. A spout could be located above the jar to pour water into it, overflow into a receptacle below and then be piped back to the spout. If the urn were next to a building or wall, the spout could be mounted through the wall. All the plumbing could be concealed. This would be fairly easy to install.

Small containers should be emptied in cold weather and brought inside the garage for the winter, or at least turned upside down or covered with plastic so no water or snow gets inside. Since they don't have holes in the bottom for drainage, they will hold rain and crack if the water freezes. Even a heavy concrete urn might break if allowed to fill with ice.

Many Japanese gardens have simple piped devices that can be adapted for our pools. One popular one is the "deer chaser," shishi-odoshi. In this device, a bamboo cane is hollowed out. One end is sealed and the other is sliced at a diagonal to form a spout and left open. The longer end of the slanted opening faces down. The bamboo pipe is attached to two posts with a wire "fulcrum" that passes through the tube nearly on center but a bit toward the open end (more of the tube lies behind the attachment than in front of it). The bamboo tube is placed just under a trickling spout. When the tube fills with water it dips forward and strikes the edge of a rock basin—making a "plunk" sound. The water pours out of the hollow bamboo cane and then the cane lifts from its own weight back into position to fill with water again.

A galvanized horse trough is an attractive container for a country garden. These troughs are usually round or oval and are about the size of a bathtub. Drill a small hole about three inches from the top to let water drain to keep the trough from overflowing. This container could be fed by diverted rainwater from a drainpipe. Or it might have a spout anchored to the side of an appropriately rustic barn. It would be best not to locate the trough in the full sun, because the water would heat up too much in summer. Algae will grow in the absence of water movement to help maintain water clarity, although water-garden plants will help keep it clear by competing for nutrients and shading the water. Mosquitoes are attracted to standing water, so as always, the container should be stocked. Several dime-store goldfish should do the trick. A stocked container will not breed mosquitoes but act as a lure and trap, actually reducing the number of insects in the area.

At Longwood Gardens in Pennsylvania, a terra-cotta urn constantly overflowing makes a spectacular feature. This idea could be adapted to many settings. A recirculating pump would make it economical and environmentally sound.

Planting the Informal Waterfall

A small visitor to the garden perpetually fords the waterfall in an elegant New England garden. Representational sculpture has made a comeback in recent years, thanks in part to the interest in water gardening.

The elevated area around a waterfall affords the greatest opportunity to develop plantings using botanicals other than the marginal moisture-lovers. Here you can use trees and shrubs along with groundcovers, wild-flowers and ferns to make a woodland setting that helps the waterfall blend in. Along with the occasional extra rock or two, you can place small rhododendrons and needled evergreens around the area. Perhaps a Japanese cut-leaf maple would also be a welcome addition. A weeping one could bend over the waterfall, adding drama to the scene.

This is also an excellent location for spring-flowering bulbs. Before the leaves of the trees have emerged, daffodils could bloom around the waterfall. Little guinea flowers or checkered lilies (Fritillaria meleagris) would look well, as would hyacinths and Scilla. Then the azaleas above the waterfall would begin to bloom along with an underplanting of blue forget-me-nots.

Ferns and water just seem to go together. All manner of ferns could be planted in the shady areas beside the waterfall under the cover of shrubs and small trees. Christmas fern (Polystichum acrostichoides), an evergreen, is a wonderful choice. The hardy northern maidenhair fern (Adiantum pedatum) is another special selection, a delicate-looking fern with whorls of segmented fronds that dance even in the gentle breeze created by the moving water itself. Larger ferns such as the Osmunda spp., including the cinnamon fern, royal fern and interrupted fern, and the ostrich fern (Matteuccia struthiopteris) could be introduced, but their large scale will make them dominant specimens in the planting and not just adjuncts to the variously planted community.

All manner of primroses (Primula) would be welcome around the nat-

The mechanical principle of the project is simply to run a pipe, usually flexible vinyl hose, from the pool up behind the starting point of the stream/waterfall. Then water is continually sucked up from the pool and delivered to the top again. It is a good idea to bury the pipe or hose that fills the waterfall, not just to make it more attractive but also because it will be protected from the elements if it is underground. Remember that this pipe will have to exit the pool at some point. This, along with electrical cord leading to the pump and the pump itself, presents problems of disguise.

If you have a pool made out of a liner, you will not want to puncture it to create a hole for the pipe and wire. Most likely these will have to come right out of the pool and over its edge. Consider a small rock arrangement to conceal them. A few plants at this place will also help. The pump and an in-pool filter, if you decide to use one, will also have to be concealed. If you are planning to span your pool with a bridge, these can be hidden beneath it (page 16). Otherwise, create a ledge underwater with a flat rock held up with plastic baskets or inverted clay pots, or rocks for the pump to sit beneath. Marginal plants in containers could be set on top of this ledge. Just be sure to elevate the pump so it is not directly on the bottom of the pool. And if you use rocks, be careful to keep all sharp edges away from flexible liners. I saved a bit of the edges of my plastic liner to lay on the bottom of the pool and for the rocks to be set upon. This extra

uralistic waterfall. These would not necessarily have to be the moisture-tolerant species and varieties; P. polyantha *and* P. veris *would be beautiful. Hostas of various size could cover the ground around blooming shrubs and herbaceous perennials. You'll probably choose many of the smaller varieties; some of the larger ones, such as H. sieboldiana 'Elegans', will dwarf everything, including the waterfall itself.*

Groundcover choices could include Mazus reptans, *a nearly ever-blooming little creeper with white or lavender flowers. Creeping Jenny* (Lysimachia nummularia) *would be a good cover as*

it would grow up and over rocks and occasionally dip into the water. Moss will look good on the rocks, and because the atmosphere is moist around the waterfall, there is a possibility to establish some of the hundreds of mosses that grow wild. Some people coat rocks with various concoctions to establish moss. I have tried painting yogurt on the rocks and pouring beer over them. I have talked to gardeners who have had success with manure tea, a brew made by steeping manure in water. And I have seen good results with buttermilk mixed with water sprayed on the rocks several times through the

season. The most important ingredient is, however, an ever-moist environment. That's either something you have or you don't.

Sometimes you can find rocks covered with moss or lichen in the woodland. If these are not in a protected area, or better still, if these come from a place destined for development, bring them to your garden. Note the exposure of the rocks in their native habitat, and try to re-create this in your garden. Mark north on the rock and set it in the same direction in your garden (use a compass for this).

layer protects the pool bottom from tearing and punctures.

The waterfall is then lined with plastic. After the levels are built up, sheets of PVC can be used to line the elevated bowls that accumulate water before it spills over the edge. You don't have to use one continuous sheet of plastic as long as seams overlap from the highest place down to the lowest. A waterfall PVC liner will be visible beneath the flowing water for a while. It will eventually become covered with algae and some soil, but in the meantime,

you can disguise it with some smaller stones. The major enemy of the liner, besides the sharp stones that can tear it, is ultraviolet light from the sun, which, over time, can break down the material, making it brittle. So do what you can to cover the liner.

The velocity of the water can be adjusted. A valve can be placed in the line from the pump; most pumps are made so that water can be controlled as it exits the pump—it shouldn't be impeded from entering the pump. Water will also speed up in small channels and slow

down in larger areas. You can have different-size basins at different levels, or you can change the volume that a given depression holds just by placing a good-size rock in the path of the water. This will make the water spin and swirl around the rock and speed up because its path has been restricted. You can also change the way the water falls by placing a flat rock at the edge of the spillway and anchoring it with a larger rock. If the water rolls over a sharp edge, it will create the sheet of water many find attractive.

WATER GARDEN MECHANICS

Although the water garden offers more interest and enjoyment for me than any other part of my garden, it requires more work. Point for point, I'd rather clean the pool filter now and then than mow the lawn, but tasks have to be done in any event. Most of the chores involved are expected, but the unexpected can happen. Be prepared to act in the event that the harmony of the contained environment is thrown out of balance. You are an integral part of the ecology of the water garden.

When I first built my small pool, I was able to create a balanced environment. In the beginning, the waterfall helped to keep the water filled with oxygen, moving and fresh. The small fish ate any mosquitoes that made the mistake of lighting on the pool surface. And the plants filtered impurities out of the water.

Much of the pool was shaded. If the pool had been in the sun all day (which would have made growing more waterlilies possible), there might have been problems from algae growth, which would have clouded the water. In sun, however, the plants whose leaves spread across the water surface provide the necessary shade. Fish benefit from the shade as well, which helps to keep water temperatures down. Cold water can hold more oxygen than warm water. Fish for our gardens, all of which are from temperate regions of the world (unlike the tropical fish of the indoor aquarium), need cool temperatures and plenty of oxygen.

After a time, the fish grew, and my attraction to the whole idea of "pets" in the pool led me to buy more. When I reached a count of five 5-inch-long fish, the pool lost its perfect balance. Fish wastes, including carbon dioxide, fed algae, which prospered. I couldn't use conventional chemicals to keep the water clear because chlorine kills fish and most plants. If your pool is out of balance, and you insist on having your fish and seeing them too, you have to turn to filtration.

A filter should be able to exchange the water in the entire pool every four to six hours. Just a few years ago, filters were gravel-and-sand devices lowered into the pool; clouding detritus was trapped by the sand. Large filters filled with such heavy material were very difficult to lift out of the pool for cleaning. Then came canister or box filters—still for placing in the water—with foam or fiber cylinders or pads that caught debris and held it until the filters were removed and washed. When my collection of fish grew to eight 8-inch-long critters, I was washing the filter pads every three days in the heat of the summer months when the activity in the pool was at its height.

This first filter was a wide tube over which a cylinder of plastic foam slid. The spongy foam, somewhat like an air-conditioner filter, strained coarse materials out of the water and held them in place with the sucking pressure of the pump.

A raised concrete pool in a California garden features floating parrot feather
(Myriophyllum aquaticum), *along with a cool retreat from the burning sun. Wisteria*
and passionflowers bloom on a trellis beyond the pool.

After a while, the debris would form a solid scummy mass and clog the foam. Then the pump had to be turned off and the filter removed and washed. A messy task, but not too hard to accomplish.

Other mechanical filtering devices are available. Some use a series of large brushes to skim debris. There are paper filters with pleated ribs to increase the surface that traps. An out-of-pool sand filter is available that uses pressure to force water through the sand. Some of the sand filters must have the water reversed to flush out impurities from time to time.

I didn't want to get rid of my growing fish, so I added another filter to the pool setup. This is a new type of out-of-pond filter that employs bacteria to consume the particles of plants and debris in the pool. It worked. My out-of-pool filter is fairly small, a black plastic box 12 by 12 by 18 inches. It is completely sealed except for the intake pipe leading from a small pump in the pool, which pushes the water to the bottom of the filter, and then it is forced up through the material inside and flows out the outlet pipe. (Because the water in the filter just reaches the height of the outlet pipe and flows back to the pool, this device can't be used to power a waterfall or fountain.) Today, much bigger biological filters are available, and although they are expensive, I would definitely plan on using one of them with a pool from the outset.

BIOLOGICAL FILTERS

Biological filters come in various sizes. Basically, they consist of a container that is sealed except for an inlet and an outlet. Inside the filter is a medium on which millions of microorganisms live. This material can be made of foam rubber with egg-carton-like points and ridges along with thousands of depressions formed by air bubbles when the foam was made. Other filters use porous rock, such as pumice. Some use large ceramic chips that resemble volcanic rock. With these materials, many more organisms can grow in a limited space because of the textured surfaces that provide huge amounts of surface area in relatively small containers.

Anaerobic bacteria will find their way into the biological filters eventually, but there are liquid additives available that will inoculate the filter with the bacteria. You can sometimes also find freeze-dried bacteria granules.

A material called Zeolite that looks like rock is used as a chemical filter to remove nitrates and ammonia from the water. It may be made of hydrated silicates of aluminum, calcium, sodium or potassium, or combinations of these. These "rocks" have to be revitalized periodically. To do this, they have to be removed from the filter, so it is a good idea to keep them in a mesh bag or similar container inside the filter. They are soaked for twenty-four hours in a salt water, then rinsed, dried and returned to the filter.

Activated charcoal is used in some filter systems to remove chemicals, organic debris, fish waste and carbon dioxide from the water. Another feature of some of the filters is that they may have a built-in method of aerating the water, which helps all the life in the pond. There may be a venturi tube. This device (named for the Italian physicist who invented it) forces water through a small opening, which accelerates it, and the drop in pressure pulls air in through an open tube and mixes it with the churning water.

OXYGENATORS

There are several plants that we grow in the pools and ponds because they grow submerged and transpire directly into the water, thereby contributing oxygen—necessary for fish. Many are also important food sources for fish. These plants aren't intended to be ornamental (however, some are). Often they have ferny foliage, which, if it can be seen through the surface of the water, is actually quite attractive. These fuzzy plants also make good, protective spawning spots for fish to hide their eggs. The plants also absorb dissolved materials in the water, such as fish waste, and help to clean the water and keep it clear.

Some of these plants are tropical, others are hardy. The hardy ones can simply be set into ponds and forgotten. The tropical ones can be harvested and brought inside to an aquarium, but I would recommend replacing these in spring when the water temperature reaches 60 degrees Fahrenheit.

Most of the oxygenating plants —oxygenators—should be planted in pots set on the bottom of pools. They also can be tied to weights and kept below the surface that way. But in my pond, with the koi, no oxygenating plant stays potted. They are tugged out of their pots by the foraging diggers. There are nets that can be wrapped over the pots to keep fish from grazing too close to the pot rims, but this seems like too much work to me. I might do it for a special or expensive flowering plant but not for the oxygenators. Also, I'm afraid that the black plastic netting might get caught in the fish gills or fins. Besides, most of the submerged plants grow quite well just drifting about.

Some submerged aquatics have flower spikes that shoot up above the water surface, such as *Hottonia palustris*, a North American native that is a bit hard to grow and nearly impossible to locate. Some oxygenators are familiar as above-water specimens, such as *Lysimachia nummularia*, which occasionally dips its stems and roots below the water, then pops up and out of the pool again to root in among the rocks of the pond edging.

The hardy plants listed below are the easiest to find through the catalogs or at reputable aquarium supply stores. Just be sure you don't introduce any parasites or diseases by buying some of these plants at a tropical fish or pet store that might be less than perfectly tidy.

Cabomba caroliniana, cabomba, has ferny, deep reddish-green foliage and is hardy in Zones 6 to 10. *Elodea canadensis*, anacharis or elodea, is, I think, the best and most reliable of the hardy oxygenating plants. It is also widely available. Fish like to eat it, but it grows fast enough to keep ahead of them. It is not beautiful, but nice enough and hardy in Zones 5 to 10. *Myriophyllum* spp., water milfoil, looks similar to *Cabomba* but is even more feathery and fernlike. It can be lovely swaying in moving water. The foliage is green or green with a deep red cast and it is hardy in Zones 5 to 10. *Vallisneria americana*, called tape grass or ribbon grass, looks like its common names suggest. It should be pot grown if possible, because it becomes dormant in the winter in Zones 4 to 10. *Sagittaria natan*, dwarf saggitaria, looks like a small underwater spider plant or a clump of grass. It is hardy in Zones 5 to 10.

PLANTING/POTTING

All water plants must be kept wet at all times. If they dry out, even for a few minutes, it could mean death. Underwater oxygenators are often sent as unrooted sections of foliage, tied together at one end. These will be untied and planted in small containers in the soil medium. Floating plants, such as shell-flower and water hyacinth, do not require potting at all; they are just placed in the pool upon arrival.

Waterlilies and lotus are planted in large containers, or in the soil of earth-bottom ponds. They need space for their root systems, and, in the case of lotus and hardy waterlilies, for the rhizomes (the creeping stems that grow just below the medium surface). If you've ever noticed how bearded iris grow, then you'll understand this idea. A thick rootstock travels in the direction of the growing "eye," the place where the foliage grows. Many of the plants you buy will come in the spring as pieces of dormant rootstock. Look closely at these sections; they have been cut off larger plants. Usually they are thick and long like a section of a gnarled carrot. One end will clearly show the cut, the other end will have the eye and perhaps some roots.

Tuberous or rhizomatous plants such as hardy waterlilies and lotus are planted to one side of the container in the top of the medium. The cut end of the tuber is right up against the container side, and the growing point faces the center of the tub so the plant will have plenty of room

to grow. They will continue to grow in the direction of the eye, and since they have been placed to one side, they have the rest of the top of the medium to travel along. The tubers or rhizome sections are placed at 45-degree angles—cut end pointing down and eye facing up and just above the medium. Then gravel is pushed carefully around the eye so as not to damage it, as described below. If the rhizomatous lily section has roots when it arrives, carefully fan out the roots in the planting medium, but still make sure the crown is above the medium and gravel surface.

Tropical waterlilies grow more like familiar perennials. They are planted in the center of containers with the roots in the planting medium and the stems and foliage above the gravel. The crown of the plant will probably end up within the gravel layer. Most bog plants are similarly planted. Bog plants and some of the smaller floating plants may arrive in an actively growing state. Often these have been washed of soil, wrapped in newspaper and placed in plastic bags.

The crown, or the place where the root meets the stem, must be at a prescribed depth beneath the surface of the water. This level is specified in inches in the individual plant portrait. Waterlilies, for example, want to have their crowns (including the eye of the tuber) about 12 inches below the surface. A range is acceptable. However, 6 inches is the minimum for waterlilies. If your pool is 24

inches deep and the container for the waterlily is 8 inches tall, the tuber could rest on the pool bottom with the crown about 16 inches below the surface. However, the container could easily be elevated on a few bricks to bring it up a bit. Some of the marginal plants are more fussy about the depths at which they are set. That's why it's a good idea to build a ledge into your pool for their containers.

If you want some marginal plants to grow in the center of the pool, for instance, a planter of graceful cattails and another of sweet flag, these can be elevated on inverted pots or concrete blocks. (The concrete blocks can be neutralized by brushing on a solution of vinegar and water, or they can be painted with nontoxic, rubberized pool paint. This paint is usually black and helps to hide the blocks.) Some material must be placed under the blocks to keep their sharp corners from tearing the plastic liner. An extra section of liner would work, or you might have an old tire inner tube to cut up for this purpose. The best choice to raise the planters would be one or two of the plastic baskets sold for planting waterlilies, inverted —bottoms up. You might need two for heavy, large containers. You can also use several and place a section of flat slate on top to make an underwater table on which to set marginal plants.

Container sizes vary greatly. Most catalogs make clear recommendations for each kind of plant. Usually, hardy waterlilies are planted in tubs that hold about 10 quarts of planting medium. Lotuses need 20 quarts or more of medium. A tub like that would be about 20 inches in diameter and 10 inches deep.

The method for preparing the planting medium in containers calls for layering or stratifying the mix. First the proper container for the plant is selected. Then it can be lined with burlap or newspaper to keep the soil from pouring out the drainage holes, or in the case of baskets, going right through the plastic grid sides and bottom. The first layer of soil can contain fertilizer. Most water plants need lots of fertilizer to bloom, but you don't want this to leach into the pool. For one thing, it will make algae grow at an alarming rate. And if the fertilizer is inorganic, its salts can be toxic to fish. Plant food often comes as tablets to insert into the medium, or in slow-release granular form. At the present time, it is nearly impossible to find a commercial supplier for an organic water plant fertilizer. No doubt, this will be remedied soon. You can use compost to enrich the first layer of medium or pond muck —partially decomposed water plants and mud, which can be gathered by the edge of a natural pond or in a bog. Be sure that the sources for these amendments are completely free of chemicals and waste. These materials should be placed in a pocket scooped out of the bottom soil layer. Make a depression in the soil and place some of these organic materials in the pocket so they will not directly

Nature has established its own ecological balance in a pond created at Berkeley Botanical Garden at the University of California at Berkeley.

come in contact with the pool water. Never use manure.

The second layer of soil should not contain additional fertilizer. When we talk of soil for water plants, we mean *heavy garden loam*, often with quite a bit of clay in the mix. A medium like this would suffocate most garden plants, but the water plants are used to being in dense, nearly airless soil. *Never use a commercial potting mixture*, especially a "soilless" medium. These contain peat moss and perlite or vermiculite and fertilizer. Peat moss is acidic, but that isn't the main problem. It and the other two materials float! They may lift out of the containers and foul the water. You could use your own heavy garden soil, especially if it has a high clay content. If you have clayey soil, then you most likely know it. It is a slow-draining soil that has a squishy texture when wet. (It's the soil you've spent years trying to amend and improve). You may be able to arrange to have your purchases potted for you at the water plant nursery. They charge a small amount for this, but if you live near enough to one of the suppliers (page 89), then it might be worthwhile for your explorative, initial purchase.

The top layer of the container is covered with about a half inch to one inch of river-washed pebbles or pea gravel. This gravel should be fairly small (about the size of a garden pea). The gravel keeps the soil in the container and stops it from floating up to cloud the water. Don't use white quartz chips or limestone —they are too alkaline and the edges are as sharp as knives. Gravel can often be bought at garden centers, and a masonry supply would be an inexpensive source. Small gravel, sometimes called "fine grit" where cement is sold, is used to mix concrete. A forty-pound bag would cost about two dollars. Rinse the gravel in a bucket with the garden hose.

Saturate the container with water from your pool, poured slowly from a watering can. Add as much water as you can, but remember, you're still going to have to be able to lift this tub to get it into the pool, so stop if it gets too heavy. The last step is to lower the pot slowly into the pool. The gravel should keep the soil in place.

As stated, plastic baskets make good containers for many plants. Some of the huge plants such as the waterlilies and lotuses have to go in containers so large that flowerpots are not available. These are often planted in plastic containers originally made for use as washtubs or pails. Smaller marginal plants can be potted in plastic or clay flowerpots. For oxygenators, it would be a good idea to place some stones in the bottom of plastic pots to help keep them on the floor of the pool.

Planters are made from compressed paper fiber or peat moss, and they may be used as well. Sometimes these large lightweight pulp planters are available from mail-order water-garden nurseries. Wooden planters can be used, but they will disintegrate eventually. You may find that a wooden crate lined with burlap will work well for a while. Do not use redwood. It can discolor the water. And never use pressure-treated wood which contains poisons that will kill fish and plants.

Flowering water plants should be fed throughout the season. About once a month, push several water-plant fertilizer tablets into the medium. These tablets should not dissolve instantly upon touching the water, although sometimes they do. Unfortunately, there isn't an organic substitute for these yet. You can wait and see how your plants perform before fertilizing if you like. If they are blooming beautifully with the nutrition supplied by the animals in the pool and nitrogen from rain water, leave them alone.

A pool can take up to two months to catch its stride. You can fill it as soon as it has been built and the water has been conditioned with chemicals (see page 54). Plants can be put in right away, but it's best to wait awhile before introducing wild-life. Then with a few fish, plants and perhaps a water feature to add air, or at least underwater oxygenators, the pool can achieve a kind of totality.

If there are too many plants, you'll have to hack some of the leaves out. Overlapping leaves will yellow and rot. You'll have to feed the plants to keep them green and growing. Too many fish for the amount of water will require that you filter the water to keep it clean of their waste and the algae explosion that all the nutrients will cause. And you will have to have a way of putting more oxygen in the small body of water.

Before you build a pool, pond or fountain, it would be wise to know as much as you can about the requirements of the plants and animals who will inhabit it. I think that one of the main reasons for having a water feature is to stock it with living things. If you are going to put in a birdbath or a simple fountain without a substantial reservoir for water, you don't have to concern yourself with the life in the pool that you introduce. You still may have to deal with the wildlife that comes for a visit, from green slime to ravenous raccoons in some areas.

If you want to grow waterlilies, your pool must be at least 18 inches deep. Miniature waterlily plants grow to as little as a foot across, but many full-size ones will spread up to 6 feet in diameter. If you are siting your pool in sun for waterlilies, remember this. You'll probably want at least three kinds of lily, two hardy ones, perhaps, and one tropical; or two-day blooming ones and one night-blooming type. You'll also want some "architectural" plants such as iris or narrow-leaf cattail. And you'll want two or more floating plants such as water lettuce or water hyacinth. However, you do not want to cover more than 75 percent of the water's surface. Put this all together, and you'll need at least a 10 foot by 10 foot pool.

If you intend to overwinter fish, the water will have to be at least 2 feet deep; koi often need it even deeper. The actual pool will be deeper because the water does not reach the top edge of the pool. (Containers for waterlilies and marginal plants have to be elevated.) So you have a 100-square-foot pool that is 2 feet deep, or 200 cubic feet of water. There are 7.5 gallons in a cubic foot of water. So this pond holds 1,500 gallons. This is a pretty good size pool, but not excessively large.

The water-gardening hobby is growing so fast that there are improvements every year. Read catalogs to find out the latest developments. You might want to consider joining a water-garden or plant society. There is even a National Koi Society.

TROUBLESHOOTING

Several problems can arise when you are replicating a community filled with disparate elements: Plants may be attacked by insects; fish can get sick or fall prey to certain birds and other animals; or the appearance of the water just may not look healthy (usually, that means algae—tiny aquatic plants). If herons come to your pool to fish, you might have to give up the fish, or buy a very large dog. Raccoons may be deterred with an electrical fence if it can be installed discreetly around your pool or the entire garden. These are daunting problems. However, the most-asked questions about the water garden involve algae and its control.

A concentrated colony of algae can turn the water so green that fish will become completely obscured. As stated, a serious algal bloom may take place when the pool is initially set up. But as waterlily leaves spread to cover the surface and shade the depths, the algae will die. Fish and other aquatic animals eat the algae, and underwater oxygenating plants compete for nutrients with the algae, and most often, win.

When the weather warms, the algae growth explodes. Any addition of nutrients also has this effect. It can come from overfeeding fish; from koi stirring up the bottom of the pool—exposing more debris and dissolving settled nutrients or from runoff filled with nitrogen that enters the pool from fertilized gardens and lawns. Keeping the pool in balance will control algae.

There are products offered in the mail-order catalogs to kill algae. Some can be used with plants and others with fish. One might harm or kill the fish, while another will kill the plants. Look for a preparation to use with both plants and fish. Be sure to read the label and follow directions exactly. (Many of these products are imported from Great Britain and deal in milliliters and imperial gallons. A conversion chart will be helpful. Often, a table of metric equivalents can be found in a good dictionary.) These formulations kill the algae, which turns brown and sinks to the bottom of the pool where it then must be vacuumed away. The condition may return and the process will have to be repeated.

There is a non-toxic pigment available that literally tints the water black. This slows or halts the growth of algae and makes the pool look bottomless. I used this product once following the instructions and it turned out I couldn't see the fish for a week. It might be useful for very small containers or pools when an effect of limitless depth is desirable. I think that the first way to control any problem is by avoiding it—keeping the pool in balance. Second, employ filters. Both my mechanical and biological filters keep the water very clear, although, our pools will never be as clear as a swimming pool. Nothing can live in a swimming pool when chemicals such as chlorine are used to make the water dead—alright for swimming but not for the living garden pool. Chlorine kills animals and plants—that's the point of its use.

Conditioning

All water must be conditioned before any fish are introduced. Chlorine will leach out of water in time. You can fill your pool at the outset and let it stand unplanted for 3 to 7 days. Because it dissipates, chlorine has to be added regularly to swimming pools. My New York City water is soft, and of very high quality. It has low concentrations of chlorine, but it still must be conditioned by letting it stand, or with a product that instantly neutralizes the chemicals. One brand of neutralizer is AquaSafe™, another is DeChlor™.

I've found a commercial preparation at aquarium stores that not only neutralizes chemicals but also beefs up the slime coat on fish with aloe vera. I think it works best of all, but I don't really know if that's true or if it just makes me feel better. In any event, Stress Coat™, with nature's "liquid bandage," is the brand I buy. One teaspoon is used for every 10 gallons of water. One cup treats approximately 500 gallons of water. I've had a few experiences, for exmaple, with water splashing on a leaf and out of the pool, which necessitated adding water in a hurry. I would have been lost without the proper preparation.

Chloramine is a compound made from chlorine and ammonia that is used to treat tap water in many communities. It is even more deadly to fish than chlorine. Chloramine will not leach out of water naturally as chlorine does. It must be treated with chemicals. If you know that your drinking water contains this chemical be sure always to treat it when you top off the pool (add water to replace that lost through evaporation), and keep enough chemical on hand for emergencies. AquaSafe™ and Ammo-Lock™ are two commercial treatments for chloramine.

A Well-adjusted Home

I have never lost a fish in the five years since I stocked my pool. Diligent attention is an important part of my success. Fish are delicate and many things can make them sick. I have heard of a case where an entire pool-full of fish were killed by fumes from an outdoor barbecue. Koi can live quite well in water clouded with natural debris and algae. They, and their relatives the goldfish, are descended from carp which are notorious for stirring up the bottom of ponds, sometimes making it too cloudy for other fish species to live. However, chemicals and pollution can kill.

Fish also become susceptible to many pathogens when they are in a stressed condition. Many things cause stress, such as rapid changes in temperature, for instance. That's why we float a plastic bag containing the fish in the pool for at least 30 minutes before introducing them to the water—to equalize the temperatures. Fish may become stressed in hot weather, because the warmer the water is, the less oxygen it contains. It is always important to run your waterfall or fountain 24 hours a day in warm weather in order to add air. If you don't have an agitating fall or fountain, think about attaching an aquarium air pump with an air stone, which makes thousands of tiny bubbles—more surfaces to come in contact with the water for oxygen absorption. Imbalanced chemicals can cause a stressed condition, as can physical handling, transportation and spawning. (Goldfish will breed in your pool, and if it is large enough, so will koi. When they are three or more years old, koi will spawn when the spring water temperature reaches 65 degrees Fahrenheit consistently.)

Stress Coat™ works well to soothe fish. It restores their slime layer. Ordinary rock salt can be added to the water to restore not only the slime coat, but necessary electrolytes as well. The proportion is a staggering one pound of salt for every one hundred gallons of water. I've even resorted to table salt in emergencies. It works incredibly well.

Sometimes, if the waterfall becomes coated with filamentous algae, I'll turn off the pump and sprinkle table salt on the algae and leave it for several hours. The granular salt is also useful for scrubbing the plastic parts of the filter system when they get covered with algae. Then I turn the pump back on and let the filter catch the algae killed by the salt. This works well and doesn't harm the fish. Never use any soaps or detergents anywhere near the pool.

I've found another useful preparation. On the few occasions when one of the fish has been injured, I'll treat the entire pool, following the instructions on the container of Furaloid, now called JunglePool™ Pond Fungus Eliminator Concentrate. It works for several fungal and bacterial diseases. Recently, one of my fish became listless and hovered near the pool's surface. I carefully removed him (or her) with my aquarium fish net (another important tool) and placed him in a bath of the solution for about four hours. He was then carefully returned to the pool, and in a few days, was completely back to normal. The new concentrated material is recommended for use at a dosage of only one teaspoon per 25 gallons of water; read the label and follow directions carefully.

A water testing kit can be useful. A good one will not only test the water for chlorine and other chemicals, but also will let you know the pH of the water—how acidic or alkaline it is. Fish and plants like water to be neutral on the pH scale, around pH 7. The scale is logarithmic; that is, every number represents a ten-fold drop or increase in acidity or alkalinity. So, pH 6 is ten times more acidic than pH 7.

It is also a good idea to purchase a book on pond fish so that you can recognize and treat problems as they arise. Many such books are available. Check the water garden catalogs, and be sure to send for the Lilypons Water Gardens® catalog. It has a very useful chart of fish diseases, their symptoms and cures.

Pests

Because I have fish, and they are very sensitive to all potentially toxic chemicals, I have stopped using any poisons to combat pests and diseases of plants in my garden. But I was ready and happy to go organic. You can imagine what it must be like to treat waterlily pests when you can't even treat the nearby grass. Fortunately, waterlilies do not have many pests. One of the most common is aphids. I find that a pin-point spray from the garden hose knocks them off, or a dunking of leaves and sloshing washes them into the drink, where my fish eagerly consume this delicacy. I do add a little Stress Coat™ to the pool when I use the hose, to neutralize the chlorine in the tap water.

You can use biological controls for some insects as well. Bt, *bacillus thuringiensis*, will kill caterpillars. This is a bacterial pathogen that does not harm any other creatures—not even the same insect in its non-larval stage. There is also a Bt derivative to kill mosquito larvae: *Bt*, var. *isrealiensis*; available as handy pellets to float in the water. It will not harm fish or any other animals, however, if you have fish, you really shouldn't have a mosquito problem, unless your pool is very large or has some shallow areas where the fish can't go.

Good housekeeping keeps trouble at bay. Remove faded waterlily leaves as often as you can. If these have been damaged by insects, such as the "false leaf-mining midge," which creates tunnels in the leaf surfaces, then continually removing damaged portions is the best way to deal with the problem. Cleaning the area of debris is also very important for all aspects of the water garden. Removing fallen leaves from the water, or keeping them out with netting in the fall, is very helpful for maintaining the health and balance of the aquatic habitat.

PLANT PORTRAITS

There are many kinds of plants for the water garden. Some of these merely appreciate moist soil for their roots, a condition that might be called "wet feet." These are plants of the bogs and marshes. Some are as familiar as skunk cabbage, jack-in-the-pulpit or flag iris. Other water plants could be described as floating plants, and most of these are called waterlilies. Nearly all of the plants we know as waterlilies are actually hybrids and cultivated varieties of one genus: *Nymphaea*. However, there are several other plants that grow in a similar way, that is, with leaves either on the surface of the water or just above it. Besides the *Nymphaea* species and hybrids, there are lotus (*Nelumbo* species); *Nuphars*, which are somewhat like waterlilies but without the many-petaled, colorful flowers; the tiny *Nymphoides*; and the enormous *Victorias*. *Nymphaeas* and these others should have their roots in soil. In nature, they grow rooted in the mucky bottom of ponds or in the shallows of lakes. In our gardens, they will be planted in pots lowered into the water to a specific depth. Other floating plants do not always resemble the waterlilies and may or may not have roots systems that have to be in soil or pond muck. Some of these simply float along the water's surface with their roots dangling.

The list of water plants that follows is divided into the floating plants (first hardy, then tropical) and the marsh plants (hardy and tropical) whose leaves and flowers shoot well above the water surface. The hardy ones will survive outdoors in the winter in most Northern American climates. Their particular cold-temperature ranges are expressed by the USDA Zone numbers. The tender types are usually from subtropical or tropical areas of the world. These are grown as annuals, to be discarded in the fall, although some go dormant and can be stored as tubers or rootstock in frost-free protected places, such as the garage. Others can be removed, pot and all, before fall and brought to sunny windows indoors, or, ideally, a greenhouse. This arduous task leads most of us to grow them for the season, let them pass on, and reorder in winter for spring delivery and planting, when all danger of late frost has passed.

All the plants below need moist soil. Some can stand the water-logged condition that develops when their pots are completely submerged—in fact, many must have this. A plant that just likes moist soil would have its planting depth expressed as 0 inches. One that wants constantly moist soil might have the recommendation of 0 to 6 inches. And the plants that need their pots submerged with roots constantly under water might have a listing of 12 inches deep or more.

One of Suzanne Bales's naturalistic pools. Ms. Bales has found that a few tropical waterlilies (for instance, Nymphaea *'Colorata' and N. 'Director George T. Moore') will bloom in partial shade.*

PLANT PORTRAIT KEY

Here is a guide to the symbols and terms used throughout this section.

Latin name of the plant is in boldface italic.
Phonetic pronunciation of the Latin name is in parentheses.
Common name of the plant is in boldface type.
Height is given as inches of foliage, not of flower; floating pads are listed as 0 inches.
Season of bloom: SP = spring, SU = summer, F = fall, W = winter; E = early, L = late, thus, ESP = early spring.
Color is given for plant flowers.
Depth is given for the distance the pot rim should sit below the water's surface.
The average hours of sun needed per day is indicated by symbols. The first symbol is what the plant prefers, but the plant is adaptable to all conditions listed.
○ **Sun**—six or more hours of strong, direct sunlight per day
◑ **Part shade**—three to six hours of direct sunlight per day.
● **Shade**—two hours or less of direct sunlight per day.
Zones: Check the USDA Plant Hardiness Map (pages 90–91), based on average annual temperatures for each area—or zone —of the United States to see in which zone you are gardening. Every plant portrait lists the zones best for that plant.

HARDY FLOATING PLANTS

Lemna minor

Marsilea mutica

Lemna minor (LEM-na MI-nor) **duckweed,** ◑ ●
Height: 0 inches
Zones: 4 to 10
Duckweed is not a delicacy of feathered friends. Ducks don't eat it, but fish do; they love it. However, duckweed is really a *weed*—a menace, in fact. It has the positive habit of creating a shade cover for the pond or pool to keep down the algae growth, caused by sunlight. However, I don't think that is a reason to allow it in your pool. Once you have it, you'll find it difficult to get rid of it. It spreads so fast, you can practically see it grow. It eventually forms a green carpet so thick you can peel it off the pond. I suppose it would make a good source of compost material, but it is more likely to clog a filter.

The way one usually acquires duckweed is along with an intentionally purchased plant. It very often clings to the roots and leaves of nursery-grown stock. It might even come inside or stick to the sides of the plastic bag in which mail-ordered fish and scavengers are shipped. A few nurseries sell *Lemna*. I think they should stop this practice, or at least warn consumers.

A plant similiar in behavior, although slightly more manageable, is water fern (*Salvinia rotundifolia*), which is worth mentioning because of its incredibly interesting growth habit. The tiny plant has ruffles upon ruffles of green leaves. It, too, has small roots that hang in the water like the duckweed, and it can be skimmed off the pond if it becomes a problem.

Marsilea mutica, and species (mar-SIL-ee-a MEW-ti-ca), **water clover,** ○ ◑ ●
Height: 0 inches
Depth: 6 to 12 inches
Zones: 6 to 9
*Marsilea*s are extraordinary plants. The leaves look exactly like large four-leaf clovers, 2 to 3 inches across. Some have color zones of brown or yellow on a grass-green background. Incredibly, these are actually ferns, ferns that float. Some are North American natives, and some are so vigorous that they have become problems in the wild. Nonetheless, these are exquisite plants, especially *M. mutica*.

Usually, small rooted plants come from mail-order suppliers. They can be started in pots as small as 6 inches in diameter. Bury small plants in the containers up to their crowns, the place where the roots meet the stems, then cover with pea gravel (so called because it is the size of garden peas). The plants will spread beyond the diameter of the containers and can be thinned at any time if necessary.

Water ferns are quite shade tolerant, unlike many of the floating water plants, However, they are not very tolerant of competition from other plants that might crowd their floating leaves. More likely is competition from fish that like to root around in the soil from which these delicate plants grow. Koi, for example, will quickly dispatch the water fern—roots, stems, leaves and all.

Myriophyllum aquaticum (M. proserpinacoides) (mi-ree-o-FIL-lum a-KWAH-ti-kum) **parrot's feather,** ○ ◖

Height: 4 inches
Depth: 3 to 12 inches
Zones: 6 to 10

Parrot's feather is a lovely floating plant that grows along the surface and doesn't need a pot in which to root. "Plumes" creep in every direction, with stems arching three to four inches above the surface. Then, their own weight brings the stems back to the water, where they will branch to send up more spires of foliage. The color at times looks silvery gray, but in the sun, glows lime-green. This is a fairly good oxygenating plant, diffusing oxygen into the water through its underwater leaves, but its best contribution to the pond or pool is that it makes a great fuzzy spawning material for fish, hiding their eggs, and protects the baby fry from predators.

Nelumbo species (ne-LUM-bo) **lotus,** SU–LSU, ○ ◖

Height: 18 to 84 inches
Colors: White, yellow, pink, bicolor
Depth: 4 to 10 inches
Zones: 5 to 10

Perhaps the most beautiful, most revered, and certainly the most exotic of all the water plants is the lotus. It is a sacred plant in Buddhism, specifically the species *Nelumbo nucifera*. Egyptians not only cherished the plant as a symbol of female beauty but also cultivated it as a food crop. Nearly all parts of the plant are edible, but it is the tuber that is most often eaten. You undoubtedly have sampled it in Chinese cooking. The root is sliced, and has distinctive holes formed by cutting cross-sections of the hollow channels in the tuber. These plants are widely dispersed in nature, growing in India, Africa, China, Australia and Japan. And, there even is one American species: *N. lutea*, the yellow lotus.

The legend of the Lotus Eaters in Homer's *Odyssey*—all who tasted the lotus would never leave the island where they grew —may not deter you from sampling the tuberous root of these plants, but the hefty price of a ornamental hybrid lotus root certainly will avoid temptation at $40 for a small section.

Lotus blossoms, nearly 6 inches across, shoot up above the foliage, up to 5 feet, in late summer. They love heat. Buds are large and pointed, opening slowly into bowl-shaped flowers. The blooms come in many colors from pure white through yellow to dark pink and blushes and bicolors such as cream-tinged pink. They are fragrant, and in the evening, the perfume can fill the air around the water garden.

The flowers, which close at night, last about three days after they have fully opened. Once the petals drop, the beautiful seed pods are revealed, which hold their bounty in chambers arranged around the flat face of a funnel-shaped pod. The pods on stems may be cut and dried or allowed to remain on the plant to dry in place for a wonderful effect. The seeds rattle in the dried pods, which are beautiful for indoor arrangements; they actually remain viable within their hard seed coats for a century or more.

Myriophyllum aquaticum

Nelumbo nucifera

Nelumbo nucifera ‘*Maggie Belle*’

Seedpod of Nelumbo nucifera

Nuphar

The leaves of the lotus are nearly as exquisite as the flowers and seed pots. They are flat disks up to 2 feet in diameter, held high on stems that meet the leaves nearly at their centers, somewhat like umbrellas. They are blue-green or green and very matte. The surface condition of the leaves is glaucous, sort of powdery. Water will not stay on the leaves. Poured onto the leaf, it will swirl around and eventually spill off. Sometimes a droplet of water will form a bead in the center of the leaf and stay there like a perfect round jewel. To see a group of lotus plants, their leaves waving in the breeze in unison, is one of the most spectacular sights in all the botanical world.

Lotuses arrive as dormant tubers, which should be planted in containers horizontally, just below the soil surface and covered with a shallow layer of pea gravel. The eye or growing point of the tuber must be left exposed above the gravel surface. Lotuses grow slowly at first. It will take about a year for a newly planted section to become

blooming size. (If you are a little chicken to try something so expensive from dormant stock, you might be able to purchase a growing plant in person from one of the nurseries listed on page 89.)

When lotuses are planted directly into the soil of a natural or man-made, earth-bottom pond (in water 3 to 4 feet deep), they will eventually colonize the entire area. In a container, obviously, the diameter of the plant will be restricted. Lotuses are big plants and require large containers. They, like the waterlilies, are also gross feeders and require consistent feeding. The height and spread of the individual depends on the variety. There are now miniatures available that will grow with flowers about 3 feet tall, so are small enough to plant in pots for relatively small water-holding containers, such as half whiskey barrels. To bloom, the barrels must be placed in an area where the plants will receive *at least* six hours or more of direct sunlight daily.

The most common method of propagation is simply to break off a section of the bananalike tuber and plant it. Place the container of new tubers (or recently planted dormant tubers) under a few inches of water until leaves emerge and reach the surface of the water. Then lower the container in the water a few inches every few days until it is down to the recommended level, at least 4 inches below the surface. Use bricks to elevate the pots and remove them to lower the container into place.

Keep your eyes peeled for aphids. The best way to deal

with these critters is to direct a gentle spray from the hose onto the plants and flush the insects into the drink where they will quickly be gobbled up by the fish. Unfortunately, koi reek havoc with lotus, as they do with many plants in tubs or pots. You can employ some kind of plastic net for a guard or get the plants well established elsewhere before you lower them into the pool. However, be advised that the rooting, foraging carp relatives love to churn up any debris on the bottom of the pond or the top of a pot, and they eat anything that seems remotely tasty. Lotuses may not have a chance, except in a large pool, where other things might distract the voracious koi.

Nuphar species (NEW-far) **nuphar, spatterdock, pond lily,** SU, ○ ◑

Height: 0 inches
Color: Yellow
Depth: 12 to 24 inches
Zones: 3 to 9

Nuphars are not often carried by mail-order suppliers because they are rather easy to grow, and perhaps not showy enough to warrant attention. They will spread in earth-bottom pools. Since they are more tolerant of colder water and moving water than *Nymphaea*, they will crowd them out. They don't bloom as much, but do put out numerous leaves up to 2 feet across. Many people find the flowers a bit dull; however, I like them. Homely they may be, but look closely. Each has several cup-shaped petals that surround a green and yellow center of frilly anthers and a marvelous central structure. Perhaps they are a little weird, but that always attracts me. (I think they would be wonderful in any *Star Trek* fan's garden.) All in all, they may be called the poor stepchild to the waterlilies and best left to large areas they like, lakes and such, where a cover would be welcome.

Nymphaea species (nimf-IE-a) waterlily, SU, ○ ◑

Height: 0 inches
Colors: White, yellow, pink, purple-blue, red
Depth: 6 to 14 inches
Zones: 3 to 10 (by type and variety)

Usually when one thinks of waterlilies it's the single genus, *Nymphaea*. But that does not mean that there is only one type of flower known as a waterlily. These plants are very variable, and over the years, hundreds of hybrids have been developed through intentional crossbreeding of species and "cultivars"—naturally occurring varieties with exceptional characteristics that are collected, cultivated and propagated. So today there are many colors available: white, yellow, pink, peach, sunset shades, red, purple and even blue. There are, however, two basic types of waterlily: hardy and tropical.

Hardy waterlilies are bred from American and European stock. The flowers are usually star shaped with numerous pointed petals held just above the foliage and water. There are often fuzzy centers of pollen-covered anthers. Blossoms shade from white, through yellows to pink, peach and red, by variety. They are a bit fragrant, and they close by late after-

noon and on cloudy days. The individual flowers last about three days depending on air temperature. Being so hardy, some kinds will begin to bloom in spring.

The plants vary in size by variety. Some spread across the water to 5 or 6 feet wide in a single season. The "hardies" have rhizomatous roots—modified stems that creep along the surface of the planting medium (the "tropicals" grow from crowns, like herbaceous perennials). The hardy plants can be left in the pool or pond through the winter as long as the container holding the roots doesn't freeze through. For this reason, many water gardeners lower the pots to a depth safely below the ice layer.

Tropical waterlilies are spectacular. With the possible exception of the lotus, these are about the most beguiling plants for the water garden in sun. Like the lotus, these were sacred plants in Egypt. The flowers of the tropical waterlilies are larger than those of the "hardies," and they add true blue to the color range. They are profuse bloomers. They are held by thick stems high above the luxurious foliage. The petals are even more pointed and upward-facing than those of the hardy types. There are also night-blooming varieties. The night bloomers open their flowers at dusk and they last until the next morning, or longer if the pool is located away from early-morning sun. The day bloomers have a schedule similar to that of their hardy counterparts, opening in the morning and closing in the afternoon. The tropi-

Nymphaea *'Blue Beauty'*

Nymphaea *'Picciola'*

Nymphaea *'Golden West'*

Nymphaea *'White Delight'*

Nymphaea 'Afterglow'

Nymphaea 'Gloriosa'

Nymphaea 'Evelyn Randig'

Nymphaea 'Red Thai'

Nymphaea 'Aurora'

Nymphoides indica

cals are intensely fragrant, with the night-bloomers the sweetest and strongest perfumed of all. The leaves are round and often variegated—green with spots, splashes or stripes of deep maroon or brown. The undersides of the leaves are also frequently colored purple or brown.

The tropical kinds can't be planted out as early as the hardy ones and are, for the most part, treated as annuals, purchased each year and replaced the following spring. Although this is an expensive proposition, it is worthwhile at least to try. Compare the price of one tuber, which will present flower after flower through the hot summer, to an arrangement of cut flowers that will have to be discarded in a week, and you can see that even the single season is not such a bad deal.

Nymphoides species (nimf-OY-deez) **water snowflakes**, SU, ○ ◑

Height: 0 inches
Colors: White, yellow
Depth: 3 to 12 inches
Zones: 7 to 10

The leaves of water snowflakes look like miniature waterlily leaves. The flowers, however, are a bit different. Held above the foliage and often fringed, they can be white or yellow by species. *Nymphoides geminata* is the yellow snowflake prized also for the brown variegations of the foliage. *N. indica* (*N. cristata*) is the most familiar water snowflake, with the white flowers that give the clan its common name. It is a profuse bloomer. *N. peltata* is the floating heart, with yellow flowers larger than the others.

These plants could be collected for foliage alone. The small leaves make a quick cover and are beautiful even without the flowers. They should be planted where one can view them close up, perhaps by the side of the pond, or in a raised pool where one can sit on the edge and examine the foliage. These plants are a good choice for small pools where larger waterlily species would take up too much space. They will bloom in a bit less sunlight than the *Nymphaea*, as well.

Try a Little Tenderness

The drawback to the tropicals, of course, is that they have to be discarded or carried over; it is nearly impossible to carry a mature tropical waterlily tuber through the winter. Some tropicals make little tubers at the point where the stems meet the parent tuber. These small growths, about the size and shape of a peeled water chestnut, can be overwintered. Layer the small tubers in damp sand in a plastic tub with a close-fitting top and store it in a cool place, about 50 degrees Fahrenheit. In spring, these tubers should be potted about 2 inches below the surface of a sandy soil mix and placed in a container of water just covering the pots.

Keep the pots in a warm sunny place. The water should be about 70 degrees Fahrenheit. Small plants will develop, and when they have several leaves, feel down and see if there are roots attached. If so, pinch off the small leafy plant, roots intact, and pot it individually. Each little tuber will send up three or more of these plantlets, which will become this season's flowering specimens. Your best bet, however, will be to try and propagate baby plants to start new tropicals for next summer's flowers. You'll have the most luck if the plants are small enough to fit on a sunny windowsill.

Remove the whole baby plant from the parent plant when it has devel-oped roots, pot it up and grow in a small container of loam sunk into a bowl of water. The little plants will benefit through the winter from some extra light, even from an ordinary, household tungsten light bulb placed so the light reaches them but not much of the heat.

Sometimes you will notice little plantlets forming directly on mature leaves. If they are slow to develop, or if it is late in the summer, you can help the process along by cutting most of the parent leaf off the original plant. Fill a 6-inch bulb pan (a wide but very shallow plastic flowerpot, perhaps 8 inches wide and 5 inches tall) to about an inch from the pot rim with moist garden loam. Peg the leaf into the soil with hairpins. Carefully cover more of the leaf with the soil until it surrounds the little protruding plantlet. Set the pot in a large bowl or an aquarium and slowly pour water in until it just touches the pot rim. Wait about an hour and then very carefully add more water until the leaves of the little plantlet are floating. As it grows, continue to raise the water level above the pot. This environment should provide the proper humidity for overwintering, and the little plant won't take up too much space. If all goes well, you'll have a new waterlily to pot into a larger container come spring.

TROPICAL FLOATING PLANTS GROWN AS ANNUALS

Eichhornia crassipes
(iek-HORN-ee-a KRAS-i-pees) **water hyacinth,** SU, ○
Height: 6 inches
Color: Lilac
Zones: 9 to 10
Water hyacinths, originally from tropical areas of the Americas, have become botanical pests in some inland waterways. For this reason, they are banned in some areas of the country and may or may not be offered by catalogs. Most often, even when they are sold at water-garden nurseries, they can't be shipped interstate, because they can become a monstrous weed if they escape into natural waterways.

They reproduce with a vengeance. In warm weather, they begin to bloom. The lovely blue blossoms are arranged on a spike that shoots out of the floating foliage, which needs no pot. After the second day, the flower spike begins to bend toward the

Eichhornia crassipes

water. On the fourth day, it's underwater, and in a few more days, a new plant has sprouted from the former flower spike—this one will bloom in short order and start it all over again.

Hydroclets nymphoides

However, and this is a big however, these plants are not hardy. In fact, they won't stand a minute of frost. If you live anywhere with winter temperatures that dip below 35 degrees Fahrenheit or so, you need not worry about endangering the ecosystem —the plants will simply die. They are perfectly acceptable in areas with cold winter temperatures, and I wholeheartedly suggest trying these plants in most parts of the country. They are very satisfying and will delight any beginning water gardener. Nothing inspires like success.

It has been discovered that water hyacinths love to gobble up water pollutants. They even "eat" some toxic chemicals. In controlled experiments in the South where the plants will grow year 'round, they are being used to filter water. The plants are skimmed off the surface of the water and composted, leaving the water free of potentially harmful chemicals. Allegedly, the composted material is also safe. There might be a great future for these "pests."

Hydroclets nymphoides
(hi-DRO-klects nimf-OY-deez) **water poppy,** SU, ○ ◐
Height: 0 inches
Color: Yellow
Depth: 4 to 12 inches
Zones: 8 to 10
Yellow flowers about 2 inches across push up above handsome 3-inch-wide oval leaves in summer. The three-petaled flowers sport fuzzy brown centers. The floating leaves grow densely in full sun. They make a handsome annual cover for the foreground of the pond and spread rapidly by stolons, somewhat like strawberry plants. They can become invasive and should not be allowed out of captivity in Zones 8 to 10. They have been known to clog waterways.

Pistia stratiotes (pis-TEE-a
strat-tee-O-teez), **water lettuce, shellflower,** ○ ◐
Height: 4 inches
Zones: 9 to 10
Water lettuce is so easy to grow and so beautiful. Although the name shellflower might be prettier, the salad reference is more descriptive. The color and texture of these floating plants, however, is nearly indescribable —sort of a flocked bibb lettuce. The "petals," or upright leaves, are thick and succulent. They are covered with tiny hairs, which reflect light and make them appear celadon green. This coating also completely repels water. The leaves can't be wet

Pistia stratiotes

with a hose spray, and they can't be dunked. They pop right up out of the water, buoyed by the air trapped in the spaces between the hairs. This might be an advantage if you grow them by the waterfall; they might be pushed underwater for a second, but they won't stay there.

In considerable shade the plants won't grow to their maximum size, about 6 inches across. Partial shade suits best, as do warm water and high humidity. In sun, the edges of the leaves may turn brown and crisp. When well grown, they are wonderful—they are usually inexpensive enough to make a trial worthwhile. If they give you trouble, don't grow them, there are too many other wonderful plants to grow than to try and solve the mystery of why the shellflower doesn't like your pool.

Pistia is good for your pool. The long trailing roots filter impurities from the water and make excellent spawning material for fish. The plants are tropical, so they will not survive the winter outdoors. I have carried small ones over floating on the water in an aquarium, just under the warm flourescent light. They don't look great by winter's end, and they are very small, but all you need is a few to repopulate the garden pool. They form several babies around the original plants, which simply float away from Mother when they've developed enough roots. Aphids love water lettuce, but they can be easily dislodged by a soft spray of water or even dipping the plant into the water; fish will gobble the aphids up, and of course, the plant will pop right back up to the surface.

Victoria

Victoria species (vik-TOR-ee-a) **Victoria waterlily,** SU, ○
Height: 0 inches
Color: Pink
Depth: 24 inches
Zones: 9 to 10
You may have seen photographs taken around the turn of the century of young couples being married in a botanical garden. The handsome mustachioed groom and his lovely be-bustled bride are standing on what appears to be a gargantuan lily pad. That is exactly what it is. There isn't any trick photography, although the photographer often slipped a wooden board under the pad for support. Victoria pads are five or more feet across! These are not plants for average water gardens. However, several botanists are breeding Victorias to find hybrids with beautifully colored foliage—often bright red undersides to deep green leaves. Perhaps, someday, there might be a smaller version for home gardens.

The flowers of Victorias are usually pink and somewhat the size and shape of cabbages. These tropical plants from the Amazon need plenty of time through the spring and summer to grow larger leaves and to flower. If you have a lot of space and a long, hot growing season—as in Florida, southern Texas or California, for instance—you could try these mammoths. The two species are *Victoria amazonica* and *V. cruziana*.

The plants are grown in progressively larger containers and progressively deeper water as they approach mature size. They are hungry, as you might imagine, needing lots of nutrition to support such growth. They must be planted in a rich medium to begin with, one chock-full of organic matter.

HARDY MARSH PLANTS

Acorus species (a-KO-rus) **sweet flag,** SU, ○ ◐
Height: 30 inches
Color: Brown
Depth: 0 to 6 inches
Zones: 4 to 10
The sweet flag looks for all intents and purposes like an iris plant with its vertical spears of green. In its original (species) state, there is not much to distinguish this plant. You might as well grow an iris, for at least its flowers add so much to fairly nice "architectural" foliage. The flower of the *Acorus* is a little

Butomus umbellatus

Acorus

brown catkin. However, *A. calamus* 'Variegata' is a spectacular foliage plant. Creamy white and green swords shoot up from the water or soggy streamside, and unlike some other variegated plants, *Iris pseudacorus* 'Variegata', for example, the coloration lasts through the season.

There are several other *Acorus*. *A. gramineus* 'Variegatus' is a nice grassy plant to arch over a rock at water's edge, but it would be lost in the pool itself. Check catalogs to find other members of this versatile genus; nearly all of them are very easy to grow and dependable in a variety of situations. They are hardly bothered by anything except, perhaps, an occasional nip from a passing slug.

Arisaema species (a-ris-IE-ma) **Jack-in-the-pulpit,** ESP, ◐ ●
Height: 12 inches
Colors: Brown, green
Depth: 0 to 3 inches
Zones: 4 to 9
The Jack-in-the-pulpits are about the most famous and familiar of all woodland and marsh wildflowers. In later winter to early spring, pale green sprouts push through the leaf litter of the forest floor or bog. Soon leaves start to unfurl and as they do, the well-known hooded spathe also forms, lifts and then nods over to protect the precious spadix, the "Jack." The markings vary greatly; most often, the hood is striped green, some-

times brown on the underside.

The most common American species is *Arisaema triphyllum*, named for its three-part leaves. There are other species too. If you can find it, try a Japanese one, *A. sikokianum*. It has a Jack that looks as if it were made of melted marshmallow, and the hood is elaborately striped and striking. The leaves are variably zoned with green and silver—sometimes plain green, sometimes terrifically metallic.

Butomus umbellatus
(BOO-to-mus um-bel-AH-tus) **flowering rush,** SU, ○
Height: 36 inches
Color: Pink
Depth: 0 to 6 inches
Zones: 6 to 9
Grassy foliage typifies the flowering rush and gives it its common name. It is the flowers, however, that distinguish it from some of the other grasslike plants. In summer for a few weeks, delicate umbels of pink flowers shoot up from the reedy leaves. Umbels are clusters of flowers that emanate from a central point much as the spokes of an umbrella radiate. If you cut one of the flowers, you'll notice that the stems are triangular—unusual in nature. The plants might look best in a colony of their kind, but they could be used to fill in among an arrangement of plants with contrasting leaf shapes, such as golden club, which blooms in early spring.

Caltha palustris (KAL-tha pa-LUS-tris) **marsh marigold, SP, ◐ ●**

Height: 12 inches
Color: Yellow
Depth: 0 to 3 inches
Zones: 5 to 8

Caltha palustris is such an interesting plant, one rarely found in garden settings away from the pond or woodland planting. This is unfortunate because, although it is known as a marsh plant, it will grow in average soil conditions. This native has a lot going for it. Lovely bright yellow flowers cover the watercress-green foliage. The yellow flowers bloom along with the daffodils and make a great combination with them. *Caltha* has an undeserved reputation for being hard to propagate—I can't understand that. It can be layered; roots form at the leaf axils, and if the plants are pinned to moist soil at this place with a hairpin, the roots will grow long enough for the shoots to be cut off and planted elsewhere. It can be divided, but the stems are very brittle and a bit of the plants could be lost.

The best means of propagating these plants occur just after flowering. Little pine-nut-like tubers form in the leaf axils above ground. These can be picked and scattered wherever you want the plant to grow. In the second spring after broadcasting them, you'll have flowering plants. If anything, the marsh marigolds spread a little too much.

Another aspect of the plants that is usually considered a drawback is that they die to the ground about a month after flowering. I think that's a plus. It leaves plenty of space for other plants to take their place. Unfortunately, the foliage yellows and is a bit unsightly as the plants become dormant. These leaves can be cleaned away, though. The plants will grow under some trees. They are particularly wonderful beneath a weeping cherry tree, which blooms at the same time. Then the *Calthas* disappear.

There is a double form (*C. palustris* 'Plena') and a white-flowered one, I'm told. These seem to be hard to come by. Try wildflower nurseries as opposed to the water-garden suppliers. All are really worth growing in the water, next to the water or just nearby.

Carex species (KAH-reks) **carex, ◐**

Height: 4 to 24 inches by species
Color: Brown
Depth: 0 inches
Zones: 6 to 9 (most species)

The carexes are very much like grasses. A reason for growing them is that, unlike most true grass plants, these sedges like moist soil, and don't need full sun. Their blades come in very unusual colors. *Carex buchananii* has bronze-colored foliage. In a way, the plant looks dead when it is alive; it requires very careful siting so that its unusual color will be an asset to a planting scheme. *C. morrowii* 'Aurea Variegata' (Zones 6 to 9) has wide leaves with a yellow stripe down the center and grows to about a foot. *C. nigra* is blue. It can spread and is one of the easier species to grow. It's wonderful to introduce this unusual foliage color into a planting. *C. ornithopoda* 'Variegata' is the bird's-foot sedge. It is a small plant, only about 4 inches tall, and has a white stripe down the center of the blade.

Arisaema sikokianum

Carex

Caltha palustris

Eleocharis montividensis

Equisetum hyemale

Eleocharis montividensis (e-lee-O-karis mon-ti-vi-DEN-sis), **spike rush,** SU–F, ○ ◑

Height: 12 inches
Color: Brown
Depth: 0 to 3 inches
Zones: 6 to 10

I love spike rush. Thin grassy blades are topped by knobs that look quite a bit like brown cotton swabs. When I was in California not long ago, the landscape architect Ron Lutsko asked me if I knew the "fiber-optic plant." I didn't know that I did until I saw it and recognized my spike rush. Fiber-optic plant is a great name for it. But this incident reminds me of the reason we learn the Latin names of plants. The common names change all over the country, and certainly all over the world, but *Eleocharis montividensis* is the same from Athens, Georgia, to Athens, Greece.

Not quite as hardy, and to me not as beautiful (but certainly interesting), is its cousin the water chestnut, *E. tuberosa* (*E. dulcis*). This is the source of the edible delicacy, and it can be grown in our water gardens. Mostly it is a grass lookalike for gardens in Zones 7 to 10. The cylindrical stems grow to about 36 inches tall.

Equisetum hyemale (ek-wi-SEE-tum hy-e-MAL-ee) **horsetail, scouring rush,** ○ ◑

Height: 12 to 60 inches by species
Zones: 3 to 9

Equisetum are ancient plants. They come from the times when mosses and ferns covered the earth. They reproduce by spores as ferns do, but they may be even more primitive than leafy ferns. There are no leaves, simply hollow tubes segmented somewhat like bamboo culms or canes. In colonial America, these plants, whose tissues are filled with silica, were used to scrub pots, and that's how they got the name scouring rush. Horsetail describes their appearance.

If these plants are located in a place they like, moist soil or even shallow running water, they will naturalize freely—that is, spread as they would in the wild. This is a cultural notation, but also a warning. If you want horsetails in your scheme, consider growing them in pots, even when they are to grow in the ground around the pool. Not only will this help keep the roots moist, it will also keep the runners, by which these plants spread, confined. I think they are fascinating plants and wonderfully stark, making a good contrast with other plants in the water garden.

Glyceria aquatica '**Variegata**' (gli-SE-ree-a a-KWAH-tic-a) **variegated manna grass,** ○ ◑

Height: 24 inches
Depth: 0 to 6 inches
Zones: 3 to 8

There are several manna grasses, but the only one worthy of inclusion in the waterside garden is *Glyceria aquatica* 'Variegata'. It is creamy white with sparse, gray-green stripes. The new growth is brilliant magenta, and that means that nearly all the growth in spring is pink. It can be grown directly in a pot set into the pond, but will do quite well in ordinary garden soil. It can become a nuisance if it is allowed to run in a place that it finds to its liking. It is easy to eradicate just by weeding it out, pulling stems and roots.

I grow *Glyceria* with another potentially hazardous cover, variegated goutweed (*Aegopodium podagraria* 'Variegatum'). I find both easy to pull out if they start to get a bit thick, and they are confined on one side by a stone path. These plants, growing in partial shade, create a brilliant spot of "sunshine" in the evening and on cloudy days when no sunlight is present in the garden.

Iris species (EYE-ris) **iris, water iris,** SP–SU, ○ ◑

Height: 24 to 60 inches by species
Color: Varies by species or variety
Depth: 0 to 6 inches
Zones: 4 to 10 by species

There are so many iris species and varieties that can stand wet feet—maybe the German bearded iris is the only one that can't. Among those that love the damp are some North American natives, such as blue flag (*Iris versicolor*) and the red Louisiana iris (*I. fulva*); and the Europeans, *I. pseudacorus*, for instance, the yellow flag which was the inspiration for the French *fleur-de-lis*. The Siberian iris (*I. sibirica*) grows in areas eastward from Europe, to what used to be called the Soviet Union. The famed Japanese species *I. kaempferi* (*I. ensata*) has large flat flowers and comes in many varieties with different colors. The Japanese iris was thought to *have* to grow in water, but it turns out to be a fine plant for nor-

Glyceria aquatica

mal soil in the flower garden, and in fact, resents wet feet in winter.

The blue flag is a familiar plant of the wet meadow. In spring, blue flowers bloom atop spiky foliage. The color varies from light blue to clear, strong blue, with white and sometimes yellow markings. The height varies, too, from 1 to 2½ feet. The red iris has narrow, grasslike foliage.

Siberian iris are not only the easiest of the genus to grow but they are among the easiest of all herbaceous plants. They will stand moisture and will grow in up to 4 inches of water, but these durable plants are, in fact, also drought tolerant. In spring, around the time of the peonies, hundreds of colorful "butterflies" light above straplike foliage. The colors range from white to near-black, with purples and blues predominating.

Usually, you'll receive a tiny division of a named variety. It's hard to believe that this little slip will turn into an enormous colony. It will. The Siberian iris seem to double yearly. Two become four, four become eight, and so on. If you want to divide them to spread the wealth around the garden or with close friends, do it early in their careers. This is an aggressive plant, and if it finds a location it likes, you'll need a chain saw to divide the thick mat that forms just below the ground. They will have a bit of a setback in the season following division (which can be done at any time of the year, but is best in late summer).

There are a few iris varieties that are grown for foliage alone. One beautiful one is especially

Iris laevigata *'Variegata'*

Iris pseudacorus

Iris versicolor

Lobelia cardinalis

Lobelia syphilitica

good for growing in the water. *I. laevigata* 'Variegata' has striped leaves, gray-green with vertical white lines. This is not an easy plant to find through catalogs, so keep a look-out. I believe that this iris may not be as hardy as some of the others. *I. sibirica* is hardy at least to Zone 4. There is also a useful variegated form of the yellow flag, but its pale yellow stripes fade to green by summer.

Lobelia cardinalis (lo-BEL-ee-a kah-di-NAH-lis) **cardinal flower**, SU/LSU, ○ ◐ ●

Height: 30 inches
Color: Red
Depth: 0 to 3 inches
Zones: 2 to 8

The clear scarlet color of the cardinal flower's blossoms out-shines the most brilliant fire-engine-red geranium in the late summer garden. Many nectar-filled, flaring trumpets line a flower spike that can be 6 or more inches tall on a 30-inch plant. There is a closely related species, *Lobelia splendens*, with deep wine-colored foliage that makes the spectacular sublime.

These perennials are short-lived, however. Any self-sown progeny should be encouraged. Otherwise, it is quite easy to grow, and although it will toler-ate full sun if the location is moist enough, it will also bloom in considerable shade. This is an American native that should be encouraged in all gardens.

Lobelia syphilitica (lo-BEL-ee-a si-fi-LI-ti-ka) **great blue lobelia**, LSU, ◐

Height: 24 to 36 inches
Color: Blue
Depth: 0 to 3 inches
Zones: 4 to 9

The Latin species name of this plant is derived from a belief that the plant had medicinal properties. Besides that, or in spite of it, this is a wonderful plant to grow by the waterside or on the edge of a wet meadow. Rich blue flowers line the ter-minal raceme, or flower spike, above the foliage in late sum-mer. The height varies, but it can reach 3 feet or more. Unfor-tunately, the plant is a little scruffier than the cardinal flower. It is also short-lived, and bene-fits from being lifted, divided and replanted every two or three years.

Lysichiton species (li-si-KI-ton) **skunk cabbage**, ESP, ○ ◐

Height: 18 to 30 inches
Colors: Yellow, white
Depth: 0 to 6
Zones: 6 to 9

Lysichiton americanum and *L. camtschatcense* are not the only plants called skunk cabbage (*Symplocarpus foetidus* is the most familiar plant that goes by this name). *Lysichiton* are very large, up to 30 inches tall with wide spear-shaped leaves and remarkable inflorescens. What passes for flowers are actually huge spathes that surround tiny flower structures. Spathes are hoodlike covers that you may have seen on calla lilies or Jack-in-the-pulpits. These skunk cab-bages have yellow or white spathes about a foot tall in early spring. *L. americanum* is yellow and *L. camtschatcense* white.

They are rare plants and quite difficult to find—mostly be-cause, unlike their ubiquitous familiar relative, they are very slow growing and slow to flower. After searching everywhere for these plants, I finally located Siskiyou Rare Plant Nursery in Oregon, the only source that I know for these plants in the United States. You can imagine my surprise when I found out that this nursery grows its stock from seeds sent by my friend Charles Cresson, author of Burpee's American Gardening Series *Ornamental Trees*, who grows the plants in nearby Pennsylvania.

The seed must be sown fresh and is viable only for a short time, adding more difficulty to their culture. And although they form clumps of several plants, they are very difficult to divide. These are great plants for the connoisseur with space in his or her bog garden. In early spring, when they bloom, they will be a major focal point.

Lysimachia clethroides
(li-si-MAK-ee-a   kleth-ROI-deez)
gooseneck loosestrife, SU,
○ ◑

Height: 24 to 36 inches
Color: White
Depth: 0 inches
Zones: 3 to 10
Most of the *Lysimachia* are called loosestrifes, but they should not be confused with the incredibly invasive purple loosestrife (*Lythrum salicaria*). The Lysimachia do spread (gooseneck loosestrife is certainly a guilty party). However, in the right place, perhaps bordered by a stream on one side and grass lawn on the other, they will fill in wonderfully. Unlike some plants that behave this way, they won't need frequent division to maintain strength and

flower power. The flowers form in summer and last for a very long time. The curved racemes give the plant its common name. All along the spike are small white stars that are really beautiful. The full effect is delightful.

There are several other *Lysimachia* species that can be grown in gardens or by the waterside. Whorled loosestrife and fringed loosestrife are similar wet-meadow plants and, like most *Lysimachia* species, have yellow flowers. The differences are in the size of the flower and its arrangement on the stalk of the plant. The whorled loosestrife (*L. quadrifolia*) has smaller flowers arranged in rings around the stem. The flowers have a distinctive red eye. The fringed loosestrife (*L. ciliata*) has nodding flowers, somewhat larger, although there are fewer of them, and they are nicked or fringed. The stalks are somewhat hairy, or fringed as well, and the plant might reach 4 feet. There is a wine-red cultivar that is most handsome—the flowers are the same. If either of these natives becomes too much, it is very easy to remove just by pulling. Some rootstock might remain, but that will just limit the numbers to a manageable few.

About purple loosestrife: *Lythrum* is an easy-to-grow plant that blooms for months. It's too easy, and too dangerous. This invasive plant has covered the Northeast and is spreading all over the country. The sight of acres of purple in summer may be breathtaking, but the plants native to wet meadows are being supplanted by the loosestrife. The wildlife that feeds on the natives are disappearing along

Lysimachia clethroides

with their food sources. Loosestrife, imported from Europe, should be stopped, but we may never be able to do that.

There are cultivated varieties of *Lythrum* and hybrids. These plants don't spread as fast as the species. But recent research shows that the varieties can interbreed with the species, and the resulting seed sprouts spread even more readily than the original species. Please steer clear.

Lysichiton

Lysimachia nummularia
(li-si-MAK-ee-a   num-ew-LAH-ree-a)
moneywort, creeping Jenny,
LSP, ◑ ●
Height: 3 inches
Color: Yellow
Depth: 0 inches
Zones: 3 to 8
This yellow loosestrife relative has few drawbacks. Creeping Jenny or moneywort grows along the ground and will even dip into the water from time to time, sending out roots at the leaf

Lysimachia nummularia 'Aurea'

Myosotis palustris

The water forget-me-nots have the sky-blue flowers with tiny yellow eyes that typify the best-known member of the genus, *Myosotis sylvatica*. This is an easy plant to grow providing it has moisture. It is reliably perennial, unlike *M. sylvatica*, which behaves more like a biennial. The latter self-sows readily and blooms the following spring, but rarely returns to bloom a second year.

The water forget-me-not can become a bit rank by summer's end, but it can be trimmed to keep it in bounds, or left to its own devices. It can be propagated from seeds or cuttings.

Nasturtium officinale

(nas-TUR-tee-um o-fi-ki-NAH-lee), **watercress** SU, ◑ ●
Height: 4 to 10 inches
Color: White
Depth: 4 to 12 inches
Zones: 4 to 9

I don't know of any nursery supplier of watercress, the true nasturtium (the garden nasturtium is actually *Tropaeolum majus*). However, all you have to do to procure this plant is to buy a bunch of the herb at the grocery store. Toss a few sprigs into the top of the waterfall so they're in moving water. The sprigs will quickly root and then grow with a vengeance. You can plant watercress in moist soil or place it in a container in the pool, but it will do just as well with no container at all. If your pool is chemical free, you can harvest and eat the cress.

The first time I tried to grow this herb, the results were spectacular. The deep green plants

Nasturtium officinale

nodes. It tolerates shade but will flower much longer in partial shade. There, it may flower from July to September in USDA Zone 6.

The cheerful yellow flowers are lovely against the grass-green leaves. They are borne in profusion along the stems. *Lysimachia nummularia* can be planted among rocks by the water's edge. The culture for this plant is simple. Plant it and forget it.

There is a cultivar with nearly yellow foliage, *L. n.* 'Aurea'; I have found it to be rather anemic compared to the species with which I planted it to make a lemon/lime foliage arrangement. However, I have noticed that the golden moneywort did better in more sun and without the competition of its stalwart cousin. Nevertheless, it would be a great plant to try in shade. It would bring so much light to a sheltered corner.

Myosotis palustris (M. scorpiodes) (mee-os-O-tis pal-US-tris) **water forget-me-not,** SU, ○ ◑

Height: 6 to 12 inches
Color: Blue
Depth: 0 to 2 inches
Zones: 3 to 8

cascaded over the rocks of the waterfall creating a soft, luxurious cover. About the same time, I thought my pond had sprung a leak. I had to add water nearly every day in the summer. I finally· realized that it was the watercress. It took up enough water each day in summer to appreciably lower the water level. I thinned the plants and the problem stopped. This is a recommendation, and a warning.

Orontium aquaticum (o-RON-tee-um a-KWAH-ti-kum) **golden club**, SP, ☽

Height: 12 inches
Colors: Yellow and white
Depth: 0 to 6 inches
Zones: 6 to 10

The flowers of the golden club appear before the leaves in early spring and persist as the leaves unfurl. These are on spadixes without spathes, similar in appearance to the inside of a calla lily or *Anthurium* without the surrounding sheath, and much larger. They are like yellow pokers about 10 inches tall. The fertile anthers are bright yellow and grow on the tops of white stalks. It is a handsome marsh plant but perhaps not best for planting directly in the pool because the season of bloom is early and short. The elliptical leaves are handsome, waxy and green, but perhaps not important enough to warrant the space they will occupy, which could be better filled by a summer-blooming plant. It would make an excellent foil to other bog plants with contrasting foliage.

Peltandra virginica (pel-TAN-dra vir-GIN-ica) **arrow arum,** SU, ○ ☽

Height: 24 inches
Color: Greenish white
Depth: 0 to 6 inches
Zones: 5 to 9

Arrow arum, also called water arum, isn't grown for its flowers, which are a somewhat insignificant and greenish white. It's the foliage that attracts. Marvelous crinkled arrowheads, about 6 inches long and nearly as wide, form at the tops of upright stalks. The leaves are remarkably shiny. All in all, it is a handsome foliage plant that would add a distinctively tropical note. It is, however, thoroughly hardy up through Massachusetts. This is a plant to grow in a pot of soil to set in water, for the roots will travel if allowed, spreading quite a distance and at an impressive clip.

Pontederia cordata (pon-te-DE-ree-a kor-DAH-ta) **pickerel weed, pickerel rush,** SU–F, ○ ☽

Height: 30 inches
Colors: Blue, white
Depth: 0 to 12 inches
Zones: 3 to 9

The leaves of pickerel rush are similar to many of the spears and arrows that populate the water garden. They are perhaps more heart shaped than some. The plants can form substantial colonies if planted directly into the earth in slow-moving water in the shallows. Leaves alone aren't enough to recommend this plant, but the flowers are among the best. They come late—summer into fall—and the plants bloom for a long time. Wonderful blue stars are borne on tall spikes above the foliage. This is one of the few very hardy, blue-flowered specimens for the water garden. It couldn't be easier to grow. Just plunk it in a container and lower it into the water; that's it. *Pontederia* likes pond muck, but will do just fine in garden loam.

Orontium aquaticum

Peltandra virginica

Pontederia cordata

Primula

and naturalize in a spot that pleases them.

Another type to try is the drumstick primrose (*P. denticulata*). These plants have perfect balls of flowers held on 8-to 10-inch-tall stems. They are usually in shades of red, magenta or lilac. There are many other primroses that can stand wet feet, too many to list here. Collect those that you can, and try them out. Just avoid the ones that you can determine through research come from mountainous regions or grow in gravelly soil and need excellent drainage, such as *P. auricula*.

Primula species (PRIM-ew-la) **primrose, SP, ◖**

Height: 6 to 18 inches by species
Colors: All
Depth: 0 to 3 inches by variety
Zones: 5 to 9 by species

There are many flowering herbaceous garden plants that can be grown in and near water. One of the most beautiful is the primrose. Not all *Primulas* can be grown directly by the waterside, but several can. About the best, and one of the easiest to grow, is *Primula japonica*, the Japanese primrose. These are candelabra types, that is, the flower spikes grow tall and have layers of flowers in whorls around the stems. They can be white, light pink or dark pink—nearly red. They love the streamside in running water or even a marshy soil. They will self-sow

Sagittaria species (sa-gi-TAH-ree-a) **arrowhead, SU, ○ ◖**

Height: 30 inches
Color: White
Depth: 0 to 6 inches
Zones: 5 to 10

Yet another of the arrowhead-shaped plants aptly named for this characteristic. This, too, is hardy and reliable, and in fact, gets along just fine in the forgotten waste places where there is ample moisture. It looks just fine there, but is elegant and well mannered enough to be welcome at the side of the pond. It may flop about a bit, and therefore might not be as good a selection for a pot in the center of the pond as, say, *Peltandra virginica*.

In summer, flower spikes shoot up. One inch wide, tripetaled white flowers with fuzzy maroon centers appear along these spikes at regular intervals. They are evenly spaced along the stem when completely emerged, and therefore easy to view in their individual beauty.

Saururus cernuus (saw-REW-rus SERN-u-us) **lizard's tail,** SU, ○ ◑

Height: 24 inches
Color: White
Depth: 0 to 6 inches
Zones: 4 to 9

The leaves of the lizard's tail are shaped like elongated hearts and tend to overlap in a mass. It is not the most handsome plant. The flower spikes give the plant its name. Tiny white blossoms line long racemes that curve this way and that, ultimately arching down toward the water. If placed in a spot where you will have access to the flowers, you'll discover that they are fragrant. Because the flower color lasts a respectable period, this curiosity is worthy of addition to a collection of flowering plants for the bog or pond with room for many.

Scirpus species (SKIR-pus) **white rush, bulrush, zebra rush,** SU, ○ ◑

Height: 36 to 60 inches
Color: Brown
Depth: 3 to 6 inches
Zones: 4 to 9

The *Scirpus* species are typically tall tubes that shoot straight up from their pots. The green ones are interesting enough, and although the flowers are relatively insignificant, they are intriguing. Little brown tufts dangle from thin stems. The disparate species have varying habits. Most are invasive, best confined to a pot or tub. *S. lacustris* can grow to 8 feet in height. *S. albescens* is striped along its length with cream and green.

The most exquisite is *S. tabernaemontai* 'Zebrinus', zebra rush. It has horizontal bands of white on green. The coloration fades through the seasons.

Scirpus

Sagittaria latifolia

Saururus cernuus

Symplocarpus foetidus

Thalia dealbata

Symplocarpus foetidus

(sim-plo-KAR-pus FE-ti-dus) **skunk cabbage, LW/ESP, ◑ ●**
Height: 12 to 30 inches
Color: Brown-green
Depth: 0 to 6 inches
Zones: 3 to 9

I don't know of any source for purchasing skunk cabbage. It is simply too common. But anyone who has them growing in their woodland or marshy area will probably be happy to let you have some. The plants are divided very early in the spring—best before the foliage comes up since it is very soft and, of course, a bit smelly when crushed. You can find the plants in late winter by locating the small flowers, which are covered by 4-inch-tall purple-brown or green hoods with twisted points at the top and clustered in small groups.

I think *Symplocarpus foetidus* is a magnificent foliage plant. Nothing has its special presence, best described as being similar to that of a cabbage or a huge green rose. Skunk cabbage makes a wonderful background foil for spiky iris foliage or in among Jack-in-the-pulpits. Don't discount this plant for its commonness or odoriferous reputation. Grow it if you get it.

Thalia dealbata (THAY-

lia deel-BA-ta) **hardy water canna, SU, ○ ◑**
Height: 36 to 48 inches
Color: Purple-red
Depth: 12 inches
Zones: 6 to 10

The native American *Thalia*, often called hardy water canna for its resemblance in leaf to that tropical plant, is desirable for its stiff, upright foliage. The plant lends a distinctive "architectural" form to plantings in water. The leaves are dull gray-green. The plant may reach 4 or more feet tall. From the tall stems, even taller flower shoots emerge in summer. These wands, somewhat like fishing poles, terminate in pointed sheaths from which purple-red tiny flowers dangle on thin threads.

T. geniculata var. *ruminoides* is the red-stemmed thalia, a subtropical relative (hardy in Zones 9 and 10). The leaves of this plant grow tall, to about 5 feet, but the wands with flowers are even taller. They shoot way above the plant to 10 feet. Red stems contrast beautifully with green leaves. These want full sun and can be grown in moist soil or under water to 6 inches. It is clump forming and therefore is not invasive like the hardy *Thalia*, so may be planted outdoors in the garden in warm climates.

Typha species (TIE-fa) **cattail,**

SU/F, ○ ◑
Height: 18 to 84 inches by species
Color: Brown
Depth: 0 to 12 inches
Zones: Variable

Perhaps the cattails are the best-known waterside plants of all. Graceful foliage bends in unison in the breeze. In summer the catkins shoot up through the grassy leaves. These wands are covered with thick, warm brown flowers. In the fall, the chubby catkins break apart into fuzzy dander which catches the wind and travels aloft to new places. These puffs are of course attached to fertile seeds.

The cattail we most often see by the roadside and in the waste places is *Typha latifolia*, the common cattail, hardy in Zones 2 to 9. There are others. A good choice for small pools is the miniature cattail (*T. minima*). It grows to about 18 inches tall and is not as hardy as the other members of the clan. Perhaps the nicest for a small pool is the graceful cattail (*T. laxmannii*) (Zones 3 to 9). It grows to about 48 inches and has slender leaves. Similar, but quite a bit taller is *T. angustifolia*, the narrow-leaf cattail (Zones 2 to

9). It towers up to 84 inches. There are other species, and one variegated variety, *T. latifolia* 'Variegata', which has spectacular linear stripes on wide green foliage.

All of the cattails are invasive and really should not be allowed to grow just anywhere. Besides, they look so much better in large tubs sunk into the pond's water. Just imagine a perfect circle of these graceful plants topped by their familiar catkins. It's the best way to have them in the controlled environment of the urban, suburban or even rural water garden.

Typha latifolia

TROPICAL MARSH (MARGINAL) PLANTS

Canna hybrids (KA-na) **water canna,** SU, ○
Height: 60 inches
Colors: Yellow, orange, red, purple
Depth: 0 to 6 inches
Zones: 8 to 10
These tuberous plants are just like the old-fashioned cannas that graced Victorian gardens, only they can grow in water. Large green or green and red leaves grow on tall stalks, a bit like corn, and similar to the hardy and tender *Thalias*. There is also a variegated canna, green striped creamy-yellow that has spectacular foliage; this show-stopper will attract visitors to your water garden (perhaps at the expense of nearly every other aspect of your property).

The flowers are large, the colors brilliant. They're impossible to miss. For that reason, care must be taken as to their placement in and around the water garden. They look wonderful in formal pools where their outrageous ruffly inflorescence contrasts well with symmetrical edging or even a sculpture or building.

The canna tubers can be dug up and stored indoors after the foliage is struck by frost when it turns black. The tubers should not be exposed to extreme cold, however, so this should be done right after the first cold snap in fall. Cut the foliage off to soil level and carefully dig up the roots with fleshy tubers. They should be allowed to air-dry for

Canna erebus

Colocasia esculenta

Crinum americanum

several days. Then pack them in dry peat moss, sawdust, sand or clean soil in a box or open plastic bag. Check the tubers occasionally through the winter. If they show any signs of drying out (usually shriveling), moisten the packing material slightly.

In early spring, pot the tubers up indoors in the containers that will eventually be set into the pool or in any pots if they are to planted in soil by the water's edge. They should be about 2 inches below the medium surface. Water and place the containers in a warm, somewhat dark place. As the plants begin to show above the soil, move them progressively to stronger and stronger light. When all danger of frost has passed, set the plants in a protected spot outdoors and in ten days or so into their summer homes.

Cannas are also heavy feeders. For those planted in soil, use a balanced organic fertilizer.

Colocasia esculenta (col-O-casia es-cu-LEN-ta) **elephant ear caladium, taro,** ○ ◑
Height: 12 to 60 inches by species
Depth: 0 to 4 inches
Zones: 9 to 10
If you have a lot of room for a plant with enormous leaves, then try this incredibly easy plant to grow. The effect is striking and never fails to elicit comment. The leaves are shaped just like elephant ears and are a wonderful light green with a fasci-

nating matte texture. They grow from large, somewhat cone-shaped tubers. The tubers are planted point down with the flat top, usually clearly showing a pinkish growing "eye," facing up. They will sprout quickly in warm weather and begin to tower to their eventually mammoth proportions.

You might be able to buy tubers for this plant at a grocery that specializes in ethnic food, for it is a staple in many countries, known variously as taro or dasheen. From a water-garden supplier, you could expect to pay $10 or more for a tuber. At the grocery, they might be as little as $1.50 a pound, and these tubers will be much larger. They are easy to harvest and store in a warm dry place, such as the basement, over winter. In late winter, pot them up indoors and water them. Soon shoots will emerge, and when the weather warms to a reliable nighttime temperature of 60 degrees Fahrenheit, they can be placed in the pool (if there is room) or next to it.

I grow mine in a soilless mixture in a large tub. The medium is made of three parts peat moss to one part perlite. This mixture is unsuitable for ponds because it floats, and white perlite is about as unsightly as anything in the pond.

There are exceptional varieties of elephant ears to try (these definitely cannot be bought at the grocery store). The violet stem taro (*C. e.* 'Fontanesii' [*Xanthosoma multiflora*]) is a bit smaller but has deep red stems and magnificent blue-green leaves. Scale and beauty make it a good choice to be placed in a pot set directly into the pond. There is also a dwarf form of the plain-green elephant ear that, because of its diminutive size, would be acceptable in the pool: *X. atrovirens*, which grows only about a foot tall. The cranberry taro (*C. rubra*) has red leaves and violet stems. Imperial taro (*C. antiquorum*) has a black cast to the leaves. The red stem taro (*C. multiflora*) is the tallest, up to five feet.

Crinum americanum

(KREE-num a-mer-i-KA-nom) **bog lily,** SU, ○ ◑
Height: 24 inches
Color: White
Depth: 0 to 6 inches
Zones: 8 to 10
The magnificent crinum, or bog lily, is a native of the American South. The petals of the brilliant white flowers are like ribbons hanging down. This plant could be grown as a single specimen for its flower, or in a clump by the water's edge. The blossoms are very fragrant. The leaves are straplike and also quite attractive.

Cyperus species (si-PE-rus) umbrella palm, papyrus, SU,

○ ◑ ●
Height: 24 to 72 inches by species
Color: Green
Depth: 0 to 4 inches
Zones: 8 to 10
Everyone has heard of papyrus, the source of paper for the ancient Egyptians. It sounds so familiar, and yet, have you ever seen this plant? Not many people grow it this side of the Nile.

Cyperus papyrus

Cyperus papyrus is a tall, grass-green plant with hollow, faceted stems about 5 to 6 feet tall. At the top of this slender channel is a mop top of 4- or 5-inch-long filaments, which themselves divide into 2- to 3-inch-long threads. It is a handsome and interesting plant, if a bit tall for most water gardens, and somewhat subject to the whims of the wind. There is a dwarf version, much less shaggy (*C. haspans*). Both versions are tropical, of course, and can be grown indoors if there is enough light and humidity. Inside, they will attract and succumb to red spider mites if humidity is low.

A close relative of the Egyptian paper plant makes a great indoor specimen, greenhouse plant and water-garden subject.

It is *C. alternifolius*, the umbrella palm. It is not a palm (nor an umbrella), but the common name does describe the rays that sprout from the tops of the stems. They are much more orderly than the *papyrus* tangle. The umbrella palm grows from 6 inches to 4 feet depending on its age. If you want to try a tropical grassy-sedge-like plant, make this one of your first selections. It is most rewarding. Although it is thought to be tropical, I saw one that had been growing in Charlotte, North Carolina, outdoors for more than twenty years—surviving temperatures as low as the teens.

It is far safer to bring the plant indoors for the winter. Place it in a bright west-facing window and set the pot in a bowl of water so that the bottom half is submerged at all times.

Sometimes when leaves get top heavy with foliage, they bend and crease in the center so that the tops fall to the water; these root in no time and baby plants form. The plantlets can be removed once they have developed a good root system of their own. When the plants flower with grainlike inflorescence, they also may crimp and deliver the seeds right down to the water.

There is a dwarf version of this plant (*C. alternifolius* 'Gracilis') and a medium-size one (*C. longus*). There is also a variegated one, but it reverted to green for me, so I'm reluctant to recommend it.

Hymenocallis liriosome
(hi-mayn-o-KAL-is lee-REE-o-so-mee)
spider lily, SP–SU, ○ ◑
Height: 24 inches
Color: White
Depth: 0 to 6 inches
Zones: 8 to 10
One of the most attractive of the bulb-forming flowering water plants is the spider lily. The fragrant blossoms are large. They consist of a strange, faceted flat disk surrounded by spiky rays that give it the common name. There are often several flowers on each plant. These might be best grown in pots and moved into view as they come into flower, then away when the flowering stops in summer. There is a cultivar with variegated foliage (*Hymenocallis caribe* 'Variegata') that adds foliage interest to the beautiful flowers.

Zantedeschia aethiopica (zan-te-DIS-kee-a ie-thee-O-pi-ka)
calla lily, SU, F in cold zones, SP, F in Zones 9, 10, ○ ◑ ●
Height: 24 to 48 inches by variety
Colors: White, pink, yellow, green, lavender by variety
Depth: 0 to 12 inches
Zones: 8 to 10
The wonderful calla lilies can be grown near or even in water. Most familiar is the huge white-flowered species. There is also a yellow one with silver spots on the foliage, and now there are exciting hybrids in shades of pink, cream, orange, lavender and sunset, bicolor combinations. Keep a look-out also for 'Green Goddess', a huge plant with variegated white flowers splashed with green.

The plants can be brought indoors pot and all, and they don't need to be removed from the pot or become completely dormant. You can keep them growing by a bright windowsill. They may even bloom in late winter indoors. However, they do appreciate a resting period.

Hymenocallis liriosome

If they are to remain in their pots, allow the soil to become dry in fall, set the pots on their sides and store them in a cool, dark place for six to eight weeks. They can be repotted at that time or left in their pots and watered. Plants dried in the fall will bloom more reliably in the summer.

They need a long season outdoors and this resting and renewing procedure gives them a headstart. They are fairly cold tolerant, but they will have to be "hardened-off." Take plants outdoors—when all danger of late frost has past—an hour the first day, two the next and so on until they can be set into the pond or beside it. If it is warm enough to take them directly outdoors, you still have to keep them from direct sun. Any foliage that grew indoors will be scorched in short order outdoors in sun.

Zantedeschia aethiopica

ANIMALS – THE PEACEABLE KINGDOM

Bringing animals and wildlife to your garden pool is fun, but it is also an integral component for establishing your miniature ecosystem. Plants add oxygen to the water. They also absorb fish wastes. Fish eat insects and algae. Freshwater clams and mussels filter water. Scavengers clean the pool bottom and sides. These include snails and tadpoles. Frogs in their metamorphic state as tadpoles might make tasty meals for large carp, such as koi, but when they become frogs (and this can take up to two years for some species), smaller fish in the pool might become food for them. Life's rhythm can be witnessed in the backyard pool.

The most common snail variety for cold water pools is the black Japanese snail. You don't need very many. They slowly slide along the sides of the pool and are especially useful to clean plastic liners of accumulated algae. The debris that the snails leave, bits of food and algae on the pool floor, will be cleaned up by the tadpoles. The predominant frog species that is sold through the mail-order suppliers is *Rana catesbiana*, the common bullfrog. This is the largest frog in North America, about the size of a Rock Cornish game hen. It is the most aquatic frog of all and will never be far from a body of water. (They have been known to catch small birds. Not so nice?) I love them. And I welcome the song of the males—somewhat like a braying cow. I think this noise, which can be heard for a quarter mile, is fantastic. In my very urban Brooklyn, New York, garden, I find this "music" wonderfully incongruous; it makes the atmosphere feel less citylike.

These frogs don't make the best pets; as I said, they rarely venture away from water. When I open the back door to go to the garden, I hear "squeak," plop. They dive into the water. I know that I have them only because I can see them when I look out the second-story window, and sometimes, I can see them lying still underwater. They believe they are invisible, and

Many animals will live in the water garden. Some will be purchased for beauty and for the tasks they perform, such as cleaning the pool sides and eating insects. Others, such as this frog, are uninvited, but welcome, guests.

The plants among the rocks and the waterfall of my pool provide color along with floating lilies. In winter, when summer's greens have disappeared, the delightful koi shine even more brightly.

they almost are. They lie very flat against the bottom, completely motionless, and they can stay that way for longer than I can stay standing or sitting on the bridge waiting for them to come up for a breath of air. Bullfrogs hibernate underwater in accumulated leaf litter, so I always leave a pile of this material in the pool in the fall.

I got my frogs as tadpoles through the mail from Lilypons Water Gardens in Maryland. About a dozen came in a plastic bag of water and oxygen.

My fish were babies then and about the same size as the tadpoles, so there wasn't any danger of consumption. When stocking scavengers, try to have one for every square foot of pool surface.

GOLDFISH AND THEIR RELATIVES

Most of the ornamental, cold-hardy fish for our pools are carp relatives. These includes goldfish and their cousins, which are hardy and hearty candidates for the small garden pool.

Pool fish are really the same as those little dime-store goldfish, only grown up. These incredibly cold-hardy little members of the carp clan can live a long time, growing an inch or more each year until they reach about one foot in length. The ultimate size depends to some extent on the size of their surroundings. You may have heard that fish will grow only so big in small quarters, and it's true. Fish discharge and monitor a chemical in the water, which halts or stimulates growth, so their requirement for food will not outgrow the environment's ability to supply it.

If you have patience, you can start off with a few pretty twenty-five-cent goldfish for your pool or pond. They will grow. Common goldfish are nearly exactly like their olive-green, drab carp ancestors. The gold ones are descendants developed through selective breeding in China to have gold-colored scales. The shimmering golden colors, sometimes flecked with white or black, make them quite attractive. These are *very* easy fish to grow, healthy and prolific—they will reproduce in your pool! Even tiny ones will develop into attractive adults, but you might want to spring for a few bucks more and buy 6- to 8-inch pond fish from the start.

Your tastes may run toward something more exotic, and if you are a true collector, you might forego the common goldfish altogether. Many of their cousins are more spectacular. Some are quite bizarre and those found in aquarium stores at very high prices are not always the best choices for outdoor pools. They are often slow-moving and fragile. These include the luxurious veil-tail with long, split, flowing fins. There's also the weird bubbly-eye, and the incredible lion-head. Even ornadas, available from mail-order water-garden nurseries, are a little bit too elaborate for my taste. But ornadas, along with the all-black, bubble-eye black moors, are hardy specimens. The black moors, however, aren't great choices, because their color makes them nearly impossible to see in the darkened depths of the pond or pool.

Other varieties include fantails, comets, shubunkins, and calicoes. Fantails can be selected for the pool. They have large bodies and flowing fins and tails. They often come in calico colors. The comet is an interesting and beautiful form of the common goldfish named for its long, flowing tail. The tail is always spread, not drooping like that of the fantail. Individuals are metallic red or orange, although less "collectable" ones may be multicolored or matt. The comets are strong pool fish, able to withstand winters, and often spawn in the captivity of the backyard pool.

Shubunkins are goldfish relatives with incredible colors. Red, brown, black, yellow and purple overlay a vivid blue. The blue is caused by translucent scales over a background that reflect the water's color. They often have a line of sparkling sequinlike scales along their sides. There are two kinds, Bristol shubunkins and London shubunkins. London shubunkins look somewhat like common goldfish; the Bristols resemble comets. They can breed with both of these and each other, of course, and often do in a roomy pool. They are strong and overwinter well.

ORFES, RUDDS AND MOSQUITO FISH

There are other pool fish. The orfe, or golden orfe, is gaining in popularity. It is a handsome fish with a slender body in colors ranging from gold to salmon pink. These fish are very active and tend to school—they look best in groups. They need lots of oxygen because of their active behavior, so they must have aerated water, and will often gather around the base of the waterfall. They have been known to jump into the falling water and, on occasion, out of the pool altogether. Orfes can reach 18 to 24 inches in large pools.

Similar to the orfes are golden rudds. These grow to about 12 inches long. Common rudds often are dull brown with red fins. Golden rudds have more colorful markings: bright red fins and golden sides with brown backs. I've been hearing a lot about mosquito fish, lately. Allegedly, they will eat their namesakes, but so will all of the fish listed here. These fish are not very hardy and will die if not captured and brought inside for the winter in harsh climates.

THE GRAND CHAMPIONS

By far, the most glamorous, beautiful and expensive pool fish are the Japanese imperial koi. I adore these fish, which I find to be playful, responsive, colorful and cute when they're small. I wouldn't, however, call a mature bruiser about 2½ feet long cute. Koi are my passion, but everyone I have ever known who gets koi falls under their spell. There are koi clubs all over the country, exhibitions, fairs and sales. A mature koi with especially excellent markings can command up to $20,000. I'm sure that's more of an investment than you had in mind, but these are exhibition koi. Less fantastic ones, and babies, can be had for as little as $3. Keep in mind that they can live for sixty years.

In Japan, where they were first bred from common ancestors of the goldfish in the 1820s, the koi is the national fish. The name comes from *nishki*, the word for exceptionally colorful cloth, and *goior koi*, the name for carp. Together they are *ni-shikigoi* or *koi*. Koi are so revered that they are celebrated each year, around May 10, the day that koi are supposed to spawn (mature koi, over three years of age, will spawn in the spring if conditions are right, when the water temperature is reliably over 60 degrees Fahrenheit). The holiday is called Boy Day, and it is when the Japanese windsocks in the shapes of fish are flown from poles. These "kites" are painted in the koi colors, often red, orange, yellow, black and white.

When you see them in pet stores, through the glass sides of an aquarium, they look rather unassuming. They are wedge shaped and like skinny goldfish in profile. Koi are bred to be viewed from above. The colors are astounding: platinum, orange, red, black, calico, yellow, white, brown, gray and gold—not the gold of a goldfish but the brilliant metallic color of the element. Some koi also have metallic scales that shimmer, and others have "netting" all over their bodies. Every color combination for koi has a specific name. For example, the familiar red, white and black is called *sanke* or *sanshoku*. *Kohaku* is a red and white fish.

My koi are not of exhibition quality (although they are nonetheless dear to me). They were purchased either through the mail or at water-garden nurseries. I bought them after staring

Koi love to eat! Buy floating pellets and you'll see them come to the surface. If you have the patience, you will be able to train them to take food from your hand.

for hours into tanks to pick the little koi who spoke to me, whose coloration was especially appealing. They were not expensive, thankfully—especially because young koi change color as they age. Pigments migrate and often the white background spreads to dominate the fish body. One of mine that as a juvenile had a prominent red head (named Lucy), now has a little red lipstick kiss on her cheek and is otherwise completely white.

To round out my collection of eight, I did buy one "display quality" koi. It cost about $50, took one year for the supplier to find and was under 5 inches long. It is pure yellow and remains my smallest fish. My other koi, all of whom were under 5 inches long when purchased, are about 10 inches long, now. They do not seem to be getting any larger. In fact, the smaller ones are approaching the size of the older, larger ones, and the yellow one seems to be catching up. I'm glad; smallish koi look svelte and sleek. Larger ones (remember, they can grow to 30 inches long) begin to look like bloated submarines. I suppose that is desirable to a countryman who idealizes sumo wrestlers.

My koi come when I clap my hands, and will take food from my hands. It takes a little patience to teach them to do this. Each spring, their trust must be renewed. I crouch down on the bridge over the pool and hold one piece of food so that it is partially in the water. Finally, a brave individual takes it from my fingers. In a few days, they all will do it. But it does take at least ten long minutes, the first time each spring, and they have to be hungry—which they always seem to be.

Always buy floating koi pellets, for then the fish will come up to the water to get the food and you'll be able to see them. The amount to feed them is described on the container of food, but it is usually as much as they can eat within five minutes, so that no food will sink to the bottom, decompose and foul the water. There are foods with so-called color enhancers, which have an additive made from natural *spirulina*. I used one of these for a while, but it seemed to make my orange koi appear the same as my red one. Subtlety might be better.

When you go away for vacation, don't worry about having someone come in to feed the koi. Feeding the koi is as much for your gratification as for theirs. They will get by eating insects or the algae that is always present. Unfortunately, they sometimes eat water plants as well. Koi are, as are most carp, bottom feeders and will root through any debris, muddying the water—another good reason to feed them floating food. And since they root around in the bottom of everything, they will often pull all the gravel off the tops of your underwater potted plants as well. Suppliers sell guards for the tops of containers.

Koi never go completely dormant or hibernate in winter, they just slow down. They look as if they are moving in slow motion. The time of their most active feeding is in the fall when they have to build fat reserves for the winter. When the water temperature reaches 45 degrees Fahrenheit, I stop feeding them altogether and do not start again until it warms up reliably in spring. If, however, they enter the cold season with too much food in their systems, they could become ill.

Koi and goldfish do not die from cold in most parts of the country. If they die in winter, it's from suffocation. You must never allow ice to cover the pool surface completely. Some people run out in cold weather with a saucepan filled with boiling water tied to a string and set the pot on the ice to open a hole. It's too much work. I have an electric heater designed to keep an opening in the water trough for livestock. This electric heater has a thermostat and cycles on when the temperature goes below 34 degrees Fahrenheit. It also has a guard to keep the fish away from the heated element. This device is sold in the water-garden catalogs, but it can be purchased for much less from agricultural supply stores such as Agway.

The koi contribute the most color to my pool, more than any plants. In fact, they are among the most colorful things in my entire garden. And they certainly are the most fun. I have little trouble choosing between the koi and, for example, delicate water clover. I had to move that plant to another water garden along with my tadpoles.

CONDITIONING

When you introduce fish to the pool or pond, you have to condition them to the new environment. After you fill the new pool, let the water stand for at least three days before adding plants and, if you can stand it, at least three weeks before adding fish. Chlorine and chloramines will leach out of the water into the air during the first few days, but every time you add more water, and you will have to do this from time to time, you will have to let the water stand. If the water becomes green with algae, seek a cure, but don't necessarily replace the water—you'll have to start all over again. To hasten the process, you can treat the water with chemical additives that remove these potential toxins. There are several products available, such as De-Chlor, Nov Aqua, Amquel, and my choice, Stress Coat, which adds *Aloe vera* to the brew. Whenever you add tap water to the pool, which you will have to do from time to time to top the pool off when rainfall doesn't do this for you, add one of these chemicals following label directions.

When the fish arrive, they will be in heavy plastic bags half filled with water and inflated the rest of the way with pure oxygen. Fish can live several days in these bags. By far the biggest stress for any fish is transportation. When you get the fish to your pool, float the bag in the water—still closed— until the temperature of the water inside the bag is the same as the temperature of your water. This depends, of course, on how much water is in the bag and the temperature differences. Thirty to sixty minutes should do it. Open the bag slowly and carefully tip it over so that some pool water enters the bag and mixes with the shipping water. Then gently pour the fish into your pool.

I have never lost any koi, either ones that I picked up and drove home or those delivered by United Parcel Service. Believe it or not, the UPS-delivered fish actually seemed to be less stressed than the ones I drove home. I think this is because they are less disturbed in a dark box than in an open box on the floor of a bouncing car. (A sign of stress is a paling of their colors.) It often helps to add some medicine to your water as a precaution to help them deal with their distress. It is this tension that makes them vulnerable to all sorts of ailments and diseases. I use Furaloid, a product that is mostly sodium chloride (salt), but new disease remedies seem to be in the catalogs each year. An equivalent antibacterial and antifungal preparation will work. Follow all manufacturer's recommended rates of application very carefully.

Common table salt itself can be helpful. Salt can create an inhospitable atmosphere for cer-

Japanese imperial koi can survive northern winters provided there is always at least a small hole in the ice for accumulated gasses to escape.

tain parasites, bacteria and fungi. It also restores the fishes' electrolytes and fortifies their slime coating, which forms a protective layer to keep pathogens out. A light dose, not for treating specific diseases, would be about a half pound per 200 gallons.

When I first got fish, however, I did lose them in another way. No catalog I ever have seen mentions that newly introduced koi may jump out of the pool. It was frightening to find that my first two precious fish jumped out. Fortunately, I was

there to throw them back into the water in time. I covered the pool with bird netting, In a day or two, they settled down. New introductions quickly swim with the crowd and do not jump out. The incident has not been repeated.

Purchasing Fish

If you have an opportunity to buy fish at the water-garden nursery or reputable aquarium supply, be sure to choose ones that are active, brightly colored and healthy looking. They should have no missing scales or wounds of any kind. The fins should never be torn or partially missing. An upright dorsal fin, the one on top of the fish, is a good sign.

Of course you don't have to have fish at all in the pool or pond. But that will most likely mean that you will have mosquitoes. The number of fish that you can support is limited. Cold-water fish need a lot of room and a lot of oxygen. A general rule of thumb is 1 square foot of water surface for every 1 inch of fish. If plants do not cover the surface of the water, you might be able

to stretch this rule to 2 inches of fish. So if you have three fish, 10 inches long, you have 30 inches of fish which could live comfortably under the surface of a 5-foot by 6-foot pool.

You can have more fish (I do). But you must add oxygen by means of at least one device for aerating water, such as a waterfall or even an air pump with an air stone, such as the ones sold at the aquarium store. Although my fish seem quite happy, it is highly unlikely that they will breed in such tight quarters. Koi can spawn at around three years of age. In spring, the females will start to appear round and chubby, or even round on one side. The males will develop tubercles— little dots on their gill covers—where their cheeks would be if they had

cheeks. On the days that they spawn, there will be great activity in the pool. Some plants will accept the spawn, hairy rooted ones such as water lettuce and water hyacinth. You can also purchase a spawning mat that the females wriggle across, depositing their eggs.

Koi breeders harvest the fry before the adult fish (and anyone else living in the pool) eat them. The baby fish are almost as small as pinheads. After several weeks, breeders can begin to see which of the fish might develop desirable colors. These are culled out of the thousands, and I hate to tell you what happens to the rest. Since my pool is overcrowded as it is, I suppose it is just as well that the fish have not had the urge to procreate . . . yet.

SOURCES

Black Copper Kits
111 Ringwood Avenue
Pompton Lakes, NJ 07442
(201) 831-6484
Carnivorous plants.
Catalog: $25

Kurt Bluemel Inc.
2740 Greene Lane
Baldwin, MD 21013-9523
(301) 557-7229
Sedges and grasslike water plants.
Catalog: $2

Haddonstone (USA), Ltd.
201 Heller Place
Interstate Business Park
Bellmawr, NJ 08031
(609) 931-7011
Garden ornaments and architectural stonework.
Catalog: $5

Lilypons Water Gardens
P.O. Box 10
6800 Lilypons Road
Buckeystown, MD 21717-0010
Everything for the water garden, including animals.
Catalog: $5

Maryland Aquatic Nurseries
3427 North Furnace Road
Jarrettsville, MD 21084
(301) 557-7615
Water and bog plants, including natives.
Catalog: $2

Moore Water Gardens, Ltd.
P.O. Box 340
Highway 4
Port Stanley, Ontario, Canada
NOL 2A0
(519) 782-4052
Aquatic plants and supplies.

Paradise Water Gardens
62 May Street
Whitman, MA 02382
(617) 447-4711
General water-garden supplier.
Catalog: $3

Perry's Water Gardens
191 Leatherman Gap Road
Franklin, NC 28734
(704) 524-3264 or 369-5648
Many plants, complete supplies.
Catalog: $2

Prairie Nursery
Route 1, Box 365
Westfield, WI 53964
(608) 296-3679
Waterside plants.
Catalog: $2

Santa Barbara Water Gardens
P.O. Box 4353
160 East Mountain Drive
Santa Barbara, CA 93140
(805) 969-5129
Bog plants and others, books.
Catalog: $1.50

Scherer, S., & Sons
104 Waterside Road
Northport, NY 11768
(516) 261-7432
Complete supplies, colocasias and giant taros, third generation
Catalog: free

Siskiyou Rare Plant Nursery
2825 Cummings Road
Medford, OR 97501
(503) 772-6846
Alpine, rock garden and waterside plants.
Catalog: $2

Tilley's Nursery/The Water
   Works
111 East Fairmount Street
Coopersburg, PA 18036
(215) 282-4784
Bog plants, fish, scavengers and supplies.
Catalog: free

Van Ness Water Gardens
2460 North Euclid Avenue
Upland, CA 91786-1199
(714) 982-2425
"The works."
Catalog: free

Water Ways Nursery
Route 2, Box 247
Lovettsville, VA 22080
(703) 822-9050
Aquatic plants.
List: Send SASE

Waterford Gardens
74 East Allendale Road
Saddle River, NJ 07458
(201) 327-0721
Good color catalog, helpful people.
Catalog: $4

Wicklein's Aquatic Farm &
   Garden Nursery, Inc.
1820 Cromwell Bridge Road
Baltimore, MD 21234
(301) 823-1335
Aquatic and bog plants.
Catalog: $1

William Tricker, Inc.
7125 Tanglewood Drive
Independence, OH 44121
(216) 524-3491
General supplies, plants and fish, color catalog.
Catalog: free

THE USDA PLANT HARDINESS MAP OF THE UNITED STATES

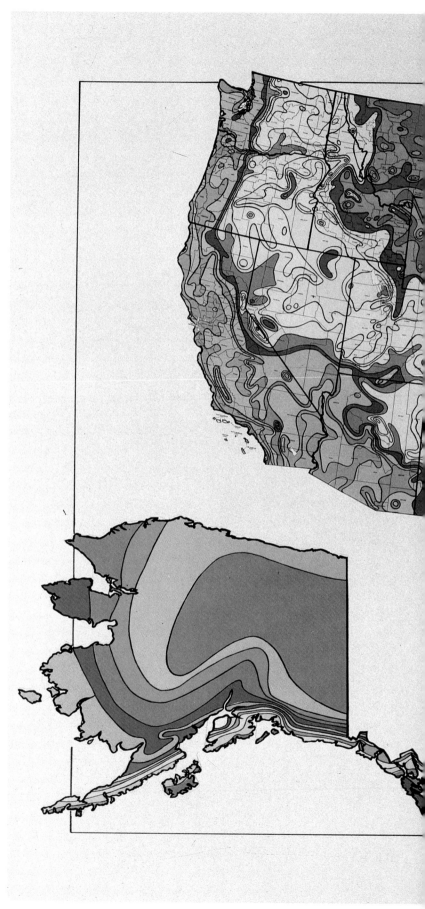

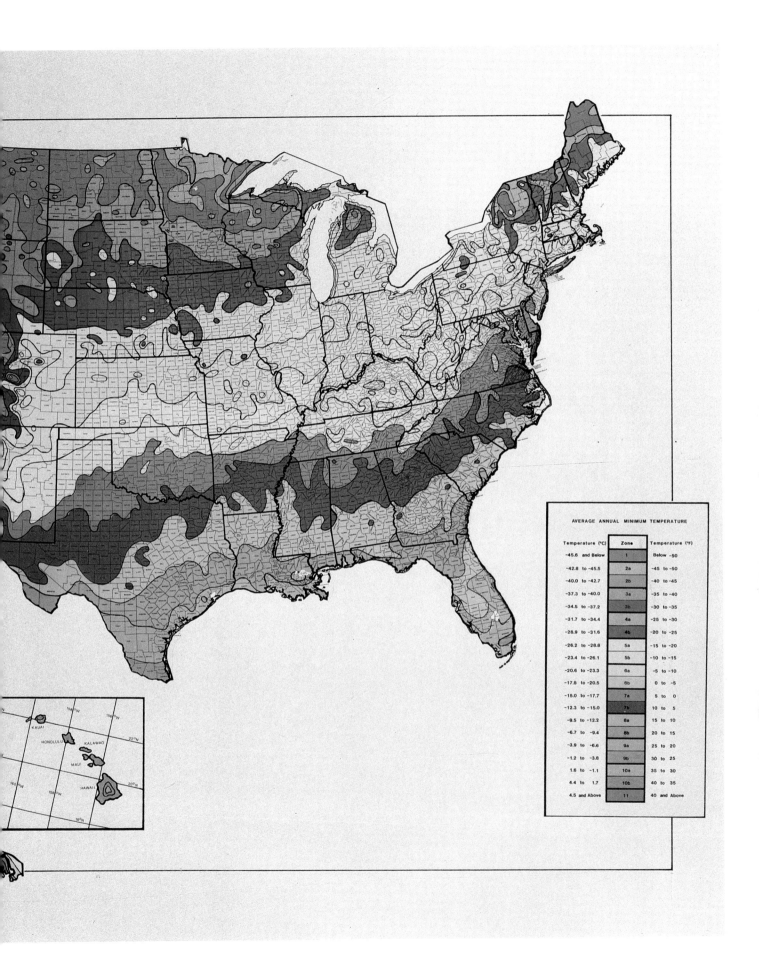

AVERAGE ANNUAL MINIMUM TEMPERATURE

Temperature (°C)	Zone	Temperature (°F)
-45.6 and Below	1	Below -50
-42.8 to -45.5	2a	-45 to -50
-40.0 to -42.7	2b	-40 to -45
-37.3 to -40.0	3a	-35 to -40
-34.5 to -37.2	3b	-30 to -35
-31.7 to -34.4	4a	-25 to -30
-28.9 to -31.6	4b	-20 to -25
-26.2 to -28.8	5a	-15 to -20
-23.4 to -26.1	5b	-10 to -15
-20.6 to -23.3	6a	-5 to -10
-17.8 to -20.5	6b	0 to -5
-15.0 to -17.7	7a	5 to 0
-12.3 to -15.0	7b	10 to 5
-9.5 to -12.2	8a	15 to 10
-6.7 to -9.4	8b	20 to 15
-3.9 to -6.6	9a	25 to 20
-1.2 to -3.8	9b	30 to 25
1.6 to -1.1	10a	35 to 30
4.4 to 1.7	10b	40 to 35
4.5 and Above	11	40 and Above

INDEX

Italicized page numbers refer to captions.